DATE DUE

DEC 0 3 1994	APR 1 2 1995
MAY 1 2 1996	
NOV 1 0 1996	
MAR 0 9 1997	
MAY 2 7 1997 NOV 2 4 1998	
NOV 2 4 1998	
	PRINTED IN U.S.A.

GAYLORD

Social work values: an enquiry

Noel Timms

Social work values:
an enquiry

Routledge & Kegan Paul
London, Boston, Melbourne and Henley

HV
3 1
T48
1983

First published in 1983
by Routledge & Kegan Paul plc
39 Store Street, London WC1E 7DD,
9 Park Street, Boston, Mass. 02108, USA,
296 Beaconsfield Parade, Middle Park,
Melbourne, 3206, Australia, and
Broadway House, Newtown Road,
Henley-on-Thames, Oxon RG9 1EN
Typeset in Times Roman by
Inforum Ltd, Portsmouth
and printed in Great Britain by
Redwood Burn Ltd
Trowbridge, Wiltshire
© Noel Timms 1983

Library of Congress Cataloging in Publication Data

Timms, Noel.
Social work values.

Includes bibliographical references and index.
1. Social service—Moral and ethical aspects.
2. Social service—Great Britain—Moral and ethical aspects.
I. Title.
HV31.T48   1983   174'.9362   82–23096

ISBN 0–7100–9404–3

But it is one thing to pursue a course of action which involves a thought, and another clearly to think the thought.

Kirkham Grey,
Philanthropy and the State (1908),
pp. 25–6

Contents

Acknowledgments

The main part of the research on which this book is based was undertaken in a not altogether uninterrupted year, October 1980 to September 1981, when I was the grateful recipient of a Personal Research Grant from the Social Science Research Council. My friends David Watson and Bob Sugden have helped me considerably by their comments respectively on Chapters 7 and 6. My wife, Rita, has read and criticised the whole manuscript. For her help in this and in everything else I thank her: and, in token, I dedicate this book to her. Without me – and our children – she would have written on the subject a better book and sooner.

1

An overview

In any discussion of welfare a term that is bound to come up is value. . . . And we may start upon our enquiry by premising that welfare consists of ordered, organised values. This, it may be complained, does not carry us far, for value seems an even vaguer and more attenuated concept than welfare. Yet we cannot clarify our conception of human welfare without some classification and assessment of those distinguishable elements to which the word 'value' is applied.

J. A. Hobson, *Wealth and Life: A Study in Values* (1929)

Summary of argument and approach

This book is about a particular grouping of seemingly ordered and organised values, namely social work values. One of its main arguments is that these values should always be considered in a context wider than that supplied by ideas of social work – social work within the context of social welfare is but one example. Much more usually, social work values are exhibited rather than analysed and are treated as commodities domestic to social work itself. For this reason, and also because I wish to argue the case of complexity in the problems raised in systematic discussion of social work values and in their resolution, this book begins with a summary of the main arguments and the general approach, despite the risk – as Moses said when reading the Tablets, 'So much is lost in the summary.'

Those writing about social work and those practising it refer frequently to values. It may be that values figure in accounts and

1

conversation in this occupation more frequently than in others, but, in my view, the frequency of reference is neither accidental nor purely ornamental. Those elements discussed under the single rubric 'values' are crucial to the conception and practice of social work. However, it is difficult to see how crucial they are, the kind of importance they have, because we try to work with 'values' as a completely undifferentiated notion. The word 'value' is indeed applied to 'distinguishable elements'; problems arise because they are so rarely distinguished. Almost any kind of belief and obligation, anything preferred for any reason or for no apparent reason at all, any objective in the short or the long run, any ideal or rule, is heaped into a large pantechnicon carrying the device 'Social Work Values – will travel anywhere'.

This suggests that while we can apply to social work values the central importance Hobson assigned to values in social welfare generally, his reference to 'ordered, organised values' may appear optimistic. The distinguishable elements fail, as we have just seen, to make obvious logical order – ideals do not function in the same way as rules, valuations differ from obligations. They also are difficult to recognise as organised. Just as the list of social work values that is treated as customary lacks coherence either as a code of practice or as a summary of principles derived from one or more traditions of practice, so a consideration of the history of social work suggests that what are usually articulated are fragments rather than the story as an organised whole. The current programme to encourage belief in the unitary nature of social work activities easily conveys interested assumptions about both 'value consensus' amongst contemporary social workers and also the unified nature of the traditions leading to modern social work. However, ways of working in social welfare and the ways in which practitioners have viewed men and women and society have often been in conflict even in what appears to be the same tradition. The kind of careful historical work required to establish such a view is exemplified in Pullan's study (1971) of philanthropy in Renaissance Venice. He warns, for example, against the dangerous assumption that 'at any given time one can distinguish a single, unitary Catholic attitude to the problem of the poor – in the sixteenth century, the views of Mendicants in Flanders and Spain differed *radically* from those of Ignatius Loyola, of Italian Jesuits' (p. 199, italics added). Historical work of this detailed kind cannot be attempted in this book, but a

consideration of three controversies in the history of
will attend to the possibility of conflict both within a
traditions of practice, as well as seeking to anchor 'value
ing historical contexts.

Establishing the vagaries of the present use and usag
work values and the disordered treatment of 'values' in cо......mpor-
ary discussion and in our understanding of the history of social work
constitutes an important set of arguments in this book. They also
mark a foundation for the remaining argument that we should move
towards a remedy for an unsatisfactory situation through a combination of historical and conceptual enquiry. The book does not
present a revised list of social work values – indeed, it is central to
the argument that the idea of 'list' should be treated as problematic
as should the notion of values that somehow belong specially to
social work. Rather the argument is directed towards a reorganisa-
tion and reconstruction of 'values' around the basic idea of practices
concerned with human functioning and development. 'Social work
values' should be reinterpreted as notions of what constitutes
human fulfillment, what aids or hinders it, what duties it entails,
what ideals it encapsulates and what valuations may be indicated in
particular situations. It is not assumed that social workers can be
brought to agreement on all or any of these elements and much
work remains to be done to save these elements from unhelpful
abstraction, but in such a perspective the importance of argument
about social work would become more clear, the tools for pursuing
argument more obvious, as indeed would the point of engaging in
argument at all.

Some possible objections to the enterprise

This book is concerned with the current status of value-talk in social
work, with delimiting some of the problems raised by such talk and
with working towards some remedy for these. Such objectives may
be criticised at least initially on a number of grounds. Talk about
talk may appear simply a diversion from more important matters in
social work; a critical approach to social work values may emphasise
at an inopportune time the deficiencies of the profession; over-
elaborate analyses are unnecessary and a no-nonsense stipulation of
how values will be treated on any particular occasion will solve all

problems. Finally, it may be objected that concern with values, whilst legitimate, is important only to those adopting a moral stance in relation to social work. These are not trivial reactions and I shall briefly discuss each of them before proceeding to the overview of the book.

The objection of diversion can be most succinctly voiced in some words of Octavia Hill. She once observed in Beatrice Webb's company that there was too much 'windy talk' about social welfare; what was required was more day-by-day work amongst the poor. Such a statement might gain recognition, even a 'knowing' approval, in other periods. There is little reason to suppose that the sentiment expressed by Octavia Hill, or support for it, is confined to the late nineteenth century. Indeed, it is echoed in the current single-minded emphasis in official circles on the inculcation of social work skills at the expense of 'more academic' considerations. The present book, however, is precisely taken up with a study of talk, that kind of discussion in and about social work which I have briefly described as 'value-talk', and one of the main arguments is that this kind of talk requires more sustained attention and more serious analytical treatment rather than the usual pious reverence or simple toleration. How, then, to defend it against a charge of diverting attention from more important activity? The proof is, of course, mainly in the reading, but at this point two main reasons for the book will be stated. First, 'values' quite simply abound in any discussion with social workers or about social work, and problems in relation to values, usually seen as moral, are frequently explicitly mentioned or referred to in a more implicit manner. Second, if, as I shall shortly illustrate, 'values' play a central role in the illumination, conception, justification and practice of social work, it follows that one of the main skills of the social worker consists in the ability to grasp the concepts involved. Social work is not just a simple matter of achieving results; it is also concerned with the manner in which they are achieved and under what description, of agent, recipient, and act. Neither 'social worker' nor 'client', nor what they are trying to achieve together (or in partial conflict), can be adequately treated as 'value-free'. In addition, 'social work values' may hold a significance for practitioners beyond the occupational. At certain times in the history of social work the values apparently realised and extolled in the practice of social work have formed for many practitioners part of a distinctive and satisfying way of life, the equivalent for C. S. Loch, for example, almost of a religion.[1] The notion of a way of life is one to which we shall return more than once in this study.

So, in understanding and in pursuing professional practice, social work 'values' are treated as and appear indeed to be of crucial significance. Yet, at the present time, a book dealing with such questions may easily be misunderstood, particularly if its main thrust is critical. Social work in contemporary Britain is a beleaguered occupation and social workers seem unsure of, or in basic disagreement about, what it is they practice. In this situation it may appear that what is required is a rallying call rather than analysis. Certainly, the present book has no directly missionary intent, and its purpose is not to ensure that the familiarly inscribed banner of commonly espoused Social Work Values (Acceptance, Self-Determination and so on) is simply and *as such* more confidently advanced. However, the purpose of questioning accepted formulations is not in any way negative; the aim is not somehow to demonstrate that social work values are either vacuous or constituted of simple stuff inflated by pomposity. The intention is to increase the confidence of social workers (and others) in their grasp of 'value-talk' in social work, though this does entail facing the fact that the treatment of 'values' in social work has been insufficiently imaginative and sharp. The book aims at a critical description of 'values' in social work, and at understanding and developing the role of value-talk through a historical and a conceptual approach.

Is such an elaborate procedure necessary? Would not all problems be resolved through a stipulative definition of 'values' so that it was immediately clear how social work values were to be understood in the particular circumstances? Usage of 'value' – to be discussed more fully in a later chapter – suggests that the straightforward, down-to-earth solution of stipulative definition has its drawbacks. In a study of the place of values in the social work curriculum, Pumphrey (1959), seeing apparently little problematic in the nature of her subject, stipulates that values are to be considered in terms of preferences, but this ignores the different grounds on which preference might be based (e.g. aesthetic, moral, as advancing certain interests, or as prudential) and the force of considerations other than those of preference, such as principle or duty. Preference is simply not satisfactory as the sole basic unit of evaluative discourse. Macintyre (1981) has recently pointed this argument by emphasising the importance in human life of the idea of reasons for action. He contrasts statements of personal preference with *every* kind of evaluative expression, including the moral. Statements of personal preference may have what Macintyre calls reason-giving force but this depends on who says, for example, 'Do this because I wish it', to whom it is said, in what situation and so on. Evaluation, on the other hand, derives its reason-giving force independently:

> the appeal is to a type of consideration which is independent of the relationship between speaker and hearer. Its use presupposes the existence of *impersonal* criteria – the existence, independently of the preferences or attitudes of speaker and hearer, of standards of justice or generosity or duty. The particular link between the context of utterance and the force of the reason-giving which always holds in the case of expressions of personal preferences or desire is severed in the case of moral and other evaluative utterances. (p. 9)

This provides an important criticism of one proposed definition, but in our present state of confusion any stipulation would amount to an arbitrary decision to exclude many different clues to the complexity of the subject of the enquiry.

Finally, what of the objection that value-talk is of proper interest to those who emphasise social work as a particular kind of moral stance; others should feel free simply to get on with the job? The next chapter will establish the importance, frequency and range of references to values in social work and the varied work 'values' are expected to accomplish, but at this point it is appropriate to illustrate that the importance of 'values' does not depend on the acceptance of a particular model of social work. I wish to illustrate, not any apparently common values, but a shared view on the importance of values, whether we are concerned with explicit or more implicit social work statements. I also hope to indicate by some brief, preliminary comment that value-talk in social work often raises more questions than it settles. This is an objective of some importance in view of the assumption that there is nothing seriously problematic about 'values' in social work: all that is required is, as Octavia Hill might have argued, their day-to-day recognition or realisation.

Explicit reference to values

In relation to explicit statements I shall briefly refer to two approaches to social work: that which sees any imperative governing social work as concern with results, and that which sees the substantive effort of social work revolving around ideas of the morally 'good' social worker and of 'good' social work judged according to moral criteria. Social work, in the first perspective, is good only if it effects some externally validated result; in the second perspective, the results of social work are seen as a moral good achieved within the relationship of social worker and client.[2]

Fischer may be taken as representative of the view that what is essential about social work is not so much what goes into practice but what comes out as a result. He is, in other words, primarily concerned with developing an effective technology, and he argues that

> Research on the effectiveness of social casework can provide a
> bridge between two of the basic values of the social work
> profession: (1) a commitment to competence and (2) a
> commitment to the scientific method. The first value . . . refers
> to a concern about effectiveness: doing everything possible to be
> certain that professional services are being translated into
> demonstrable benefits for clients. The second value . . . refers to
> the belief that a process of rational, systematic and orderly
> enquiry is the best way yet devised by man to organise,
> understand and accumulate knowledge. (1976, p. 5)

This passage uses a term often referred to in informal discussions of social work values, commitment, but to what social workers may be committed is at least mentioned. Simple references to commitment to social work or to social work values have to be pursued. Simply saying that 'social workers are or should be committed' or that 'they should or do feel commitment' conveys no information at all. One is always committed to a particular belief or set of beliefs, and some specification of these is required before we can know whether or not someone is 'committed'. Commitment to a person, from which social work usage probably derives, depends on some relevant specification of the person in question. It is doubtful whether the two beliefs selected by Fischer would be generally accepted by social workers as 'basic', but this is not the place to develop that argument. His words stand here as an illustration of the importance of 'values' in an orientation to social work that is largely instrumental.

Social work as a morally serious project has, of course, a comparatively lengthy history. It is not surprising that 'values' usually qualified as 'moral' are acknowledged, but the extent to which they are explicitly depicted is perhaps surprising in view of the frequent mistaken association of moral seriousness with the moralistic approach of an earlier social welfare. The view of social work as a moral, rather than scientific or technical enterprise, takes two forms, but in either the crucial role of 'values' is evident. First, the primary concern is seen to reside in the development of a distinctive moral character. This is more usually considered in terms of the social worker, but it is difficult to see why the distinctive moral character should not logically also be developed in clients. Hugman (1977) proposes, in an exhortatory passage, that

> the business of being a good helper is essentially bound up with being a good person, that is to say, thoughtful, generous, sensitive, relatively unselfish, relatively accepting of self, liberated in spirit, tolerant, reliable, acquainted with weakness and inconsistency, caring, committed, purposeful, capable of joy and sadness, and faithful to a belief in the humanity of all people.

This passage raises, of course, a number of questions: how, for example, can we tell that the moral character has been fully described, and how can the ambiguity be resolved in 'the business of being a good helper is essentially bound up with being a good person'? (This means either that being a good helper is connected in important ways with being a good person or that to be a good person *is* to be a good helper.)

Second, social work is viewed as concerned

> to make and assist in the making of moral judgments in ways that are directly helpful to clients and citizens that 'do good' . . . Clients need to be helped to apply ethical principles in the consideration and discussion of reasons and evidence. . . . Admittedly, people need resources to allow responsible choices. Along with essential material and social resources that social workers make available, they also need to make available the value system and ethical principles that can aid clients to resolve

their dilemmas. This calls for a focus with clients on their philosophic beliefs and value commitments or conflicts, and direct aid to them in clarifying and choosing adaptive and positive, self-fulfilling philosophies and life styles. (Siporin, 1975, p. 88)

The passage from Siporin contains a number of complex ideas. How are people assisted in the making of moral judgments in general, and in particular that set of judgments identified as of direct help or as doing good? What is the good that moral judgments accomplish? What counts as a value system? How do social workers actually make *available* a value system? How do we identify philosophies and life styles as adaptive, positive, self-fulfilling? These questions are not intended as some kind of dismissal, but as indicating the important issues raised by giving moral judgments and moralising (in a non-pejorative sense) a central place in the practice and the justification of social work. It is clear at least that this is the place Siporin believes they should occupy.

Implicit reference to 'value problems'

So far we have been concerned with illustrating the central role of values in explicit formulations of a social work approach. It is also the case that 'values' or 'moral values' or 'moral judgments' – and at present we can treat these collectively – feature implicitly in all kinds of discussions of social work problems. Space permits only brief illustrations, but again from two rather different perspectives. First, a Marxist considers some problems arising from the possibility of 'using social work as a political platform'. Second, a writer looks at certain sexual problems in residential care. In both the pressing nature of 'morality' is clear: both use a notion of 'genuine' morality contrasted with other kinds, but in neither case is it clear what this is.
   Simpkin (1979) urges that

It does not take much observation to see how often clients' opinions and values falling within a conventional range gain acceptance and approval, while more unusual attitudes meet with silence, surprise or reproval. . . . Most radicals lean over backwards to avoid pushing their views on to clients, because we value freedom. (p. 150)

Toleration, of course, has its limits, otherwise it would be indifference.

> As a Marxist social worker I am prepared to offer personal assistance to anybody provided my help is not going to be used to oppress others. If I find that person repugnant by temperament or belief I will refer them on. It does not happen very often ['Why not?' is a serious question]. Membership of a party like the National Front is not, however, compatible with social work, because of the associated assumption that some of our clients are inferior and should be repatriated. . . . Nor should we let racialist remarks by our clients pass without comment, since silence only confers respectability and prolongs prejudice. (p. 151)

This last suggestion would certainly clash with some understandings of the principle of acceptance (discussed in a later chapter), but it is also worth raising questions concerning the grounds on which one particular prejudice (amongst many) is singled out for a direct response and the grounds on which temperaments or beliefs are judged repugnant (or non-preferred). These questions are complex, but at this point the two passages are used (a) to illustrate the ordinary ways in which 'value' problems appear in social work writing; (b) the frequency with which a group of problems most would describe as moral arise; and (c) the extent to which moral values are indiscriminately listed with those that are not *necessarily* so ('joy' in Hugman, 'repugnance' in Simpkin, for example).

The second illustration of questions of 'value' arising in an unselfconscious way is taken from a discussion of a subject that is receiving increasing attention: sex and social work. Davis (1975) discusses the case of a residential assistant who was prevailed on by a resident to masturbate him from time to time. This provoked a range of staff reactions 'from uncompromising condemnation to sympathetic approval'. Davis then discusses the general approach social workers ought to adopt towards the natural physical and emotional inclinations of residents. In particular social workers should defend residents against those 'whose own anxieties, irregularly constructed moral codes or panic at the strength of their own feelings brings about a climate of suspicion and guilt'. Such a view is obviously substantively controversial, but at this stage in the argument we need to note assumptions concerning the regular and irregular ways in which moral codes are constructed (and the assumption that they are individually *constructed*) and the belief that guilt is in some sense as undesirable a feature of the climate as suspicion.

So far I have attempted to demonstrate the general and agreed view, based on explicit and implicit reference in social work writing, that 'values' (whatever they may be) and what people term problems in the value realm figure centrally in social work conceived in a number of different ways. I have so far left the meaning of 'value' and 'values' unexplored, but I have tried to suggest some of the practical and logical problems to which even brief and apparently straightforward statements give rise. The different functions 'values' perform in social work will be considered in Chapter 2, which is also concerned to demonstrate the failure in social work to treat 'values' systematically, or sometimes indeed to treat them at all. Such a failure is not acceptable, and the major part of the book is taken up with considering ways of remedying the situation through conceptual and historical enquiry. Chapter 3 presents a preliminary conceptual analysis of conscience and moral conscience in social work. Chapter 4 criticises the usual 'list' approach to social work values and reconsiders some of the main 'traditional' values with a view to resolving some of their more problematic features. The next chapter briefly reviews three major controversies in social work, and Chapters 6 and 7 consider aspects of the treatment of values in areas outside social work. The remainder of this overview sets these topics within the major arguments of the book. The topics of Chapters 3 to 7 were selected to assist in the exploration of two themes: values and practice and values in context.

Values and practice

One of the two most cogent and persuasive criticisms of the current treatment of social work values concerns its distance from the *locus* of practice. (The other criticism of ahistorical and non-contextual treatment is taken up in the next section). Admittedly, some of the usual, publicly avowed 'values' do not present problems of great abstraction: confidentiality, for instance, is not, as we shall see, without problems, but as a rule or set of rules governing certain aspects of a practice it is reasonably straightforward and concrete. It is different with other values. Statements that the values of social work are essentially democratic are at a high level of abstraction, and discussion of the idea of self-determination, for example, seems often remote from practice. This feature of value-talk poses at least two major problems: can the process or procedure be identified whereby we can move from the high levels of abstraction to the concrete details of practice; or, should we simply recognise values as persuasive slogans or legitimating cover for all kinds of activity that are in no obvious way connected to the values?

The first problem has been recognised, at least to an extent in the literature. Lewis, for example (in Mullen and Dumpson, 1972), has described one possible picture of the progression from high principle to ordinary guidelines:

> Values traverse a set of ordered levels through which they are transformed from beliefs to practice guides in professional activities. These levels are conveniently labelled in terms of what they require from the social worker who seeks to implement them. The level furthest from action is the set of *values* themselves, which designate a moral perspective. A step closer to action are the *ethical imperatives* formulating behavioural requirements through which the values may be realised. Still closer to action are commendations, incorporated in principles, which specify how imperatives are to be applied. Finally, closest to action are *commands*, codified into rules which are based on principles.

The picture of progression presented here is not, however, very clear, and the weakness in the central idea of level is exposed in what the author calls 'commendations' which 'specify how imperatives are to be applied'. Rules of conduct (rather than the more personal imperative or command) are an important ingredient of practice, as I have already indicated in the reference to confidentiality, and describing the manner of their application, the spirit in which they are to be carried out, is also important (a mere list of rules would hardly constitute a practice). Yet this manner or spirit surely characterises the whole practice; it is not best viewed as lodged simply near the sharp end of action. The analysis of certain key values in Chapter 4 proceeds not by way of levels but through closer attention to espoused values so that their implications for action and their place in a context is better appreciated. Not only are 'value' and 'values' used in different ways in social work, but distinct strands of meaning can be detected within what is usually presented as a single value. A good example of this is the value 'client self-determination', which can usefully be considered as an amalgam of norms about the boundaries of a social worker's authority, a stipulation that certain rights are not surrendered simply through the action of becoming a social worker's client, and a rather loosely argued anti-determinist position. Failure to distinguish at least this minimum differentiation accounts for many of the apparent difficulties in the use of what has come to be seen as a troublesome concept.

The second problem contained in the criticism of abstraction concerns the relationship of 'values' to behaviour. Are values persuasive slogans providing heart and 'cover' for all kinds of activity, or do they permeate in different ways the fabric of practice? Clearly, empirical research has a contribution to make, but, as we shall see in Chapter 2, empirical work that proceeds without conceptual exploration and clarification proves an uncertain guide. The present study is not based on direct field enquiry, but the problem of the relationship between 'values' and practical activity is approached in two ways. First, as we have said, some of the key social work values are analysed with a view to assessing their implications for a frame of action. Second, special attention is paid to a conceptual analysis of conscience in social work, since this bears upon certain crucial aspects of the question consistently posed to the individual social worker: what ought I to do in this or that particular situation? Obviously, Chapter 3 cannot answer that question for each social worker, but some of the important dimensions of a general answer are at least explored. Talk of 'values' easily carries the assumption that 'things' called 'values', and indeed 'disvalues', inhabit the world of real objects and that with a little persistence they might actually be embraced. Continual reference to 'values' and 'disvalues' makes them real, whereas it is *people* who make valuations and value judgments, who order positively evaluated choices in some form of hierarchy of preference, who strive to create situations of certain kinds because they exhibit valuable qualities or qualities they appreciate. So, one aspect of the enquiry must be the practising social worker concerned to act in a moral way in the given circumstances.

Values in context

The other persuasive criticism of the usual treatment of social work values to which reference has already been made concerns the parochial and ahistorical perspective commonly used. The topics already listed address this problem in two ways. First, a preliminary study is made of three important controversies in social work on the grounds that the elements contained in 'values' are likely to be emphasised and hence more clearly visible at times of public confrontation.

Controversies are not easy to find in social work. The literature of social work records, on the whole, the steady, rather heedless accumulation of ideas and findings rather than significant refutation, conspicuous rifts or the formation of schools. However, at three different times at least in the history of modern social work, strong support and opposition has openly centred on significant arguments about the nature of social work. These are the controversies surrounding the ideas of leading figures in the Charity Organisation Society at the turn of the nineteenth century; the dispute pre– and post–Second World War between the Diagnostic and the Functionalist schools in America; and the current emerging debate about the possibility and legitimacy of social work that is radical and more particularly Marxist. The objective in considering these controversies is not to present a detailed history, still less to try somehow to declare winners and losers, but to see how far these controversies are essentially value conflicts, and what 'values' are at issue and at stake.

The second approach to meeting criticisms that social work values are normally discussed outside any context at all, other than that provided by social work itself, is followed in Chapters 6 and 7. These chapters seek to illuminate the treatment of values 'outside' social work – in ordinary language, economics, sociology and philosophy.

Some preliminary exploration of these potential sources of insight is undertaken, but the potential scope of this interdisciplinary approach is considerable. In this connection it is important to recall the purposes of those particular chapters in the overall argument. Some brave souls believe that a general theory of value can be constructed. They may be correct – results will show – but the present book has more modest aims: to discover if uses of 'value' and 'values' in forms of discourse other than that of social work can help us towards a more firm grasp on value-talk within social work. The objective is to seek further insight into 'those *distinguishable* elements to which the word "value" is applied' (italics added to the passage from Hobson at the beginning of this chapter). These two chapters do not assume that there exists outside social work some perfect use of 'value' and 'values' that can simply be applied for the effective remedy of ills in social work. As we shall see, in disciplines outside social work 'value' and 'values' often receive a far from unambiguous treatment. Such rough handling, however, contains lessons for those who have adopted a somewhat precious attitude towards those values that are especially described as social work values. We shall see, in the section on the Functionalist School of social work (Chapter 5), how support grew for the view that social work values were intrinsically so difficult to describe, were of such intricate delicacy that statements attempting to capture them suffered inescapable faults. For some at least of the Functionalists there was no avoiding the fact that such statements were irredeemably vague and incorrigibly obscure. This may prove to be the case, but at the conclusion rather than the beginning of any enquiry. Chapters 6 and 7 simply insist, with Ruskin, that the right to be obscure has to be won. Before we can accept as rightful the obscurity of statements about social work values more work has to be done, and these chapters suggest that some at least of this work should be done from an inter-disciplinary basis.

2

The function and treatment of 'values' in social work

Elaine went and bought a *Guardian*, to push into his jacket pocket. 'For your lively mind,' she said, 'You mustn't forget to take your values with you.'

Malcolm Bradbury, *Stepping Westwards*

A man's values are like his kidneys; he rarely knows he has any until they are upset.

R. Huws Jones, 'Social values and social work education', in
K. A. Kendall (ed.) (1970)

The first chapter was concerned to establish the importance of 'values' in social work, but only in the most general way. This chapter seeks to demonstrate the different points in the structure of social work in which 'values' have been placed. In other words, the argument advances beyond stating that 'values' are important in the practice and discussion of social work and begins to explore the kind of importance they have been accorded. Some of the problems arising from the location will be discussed, and the main ways in which 'values' have been systematically treated in the literature of social work will be reviewed. Goldstein (1973, p. 90) has described the social worker as a 'value laden individual', and the literature of social work can be shown to labour under a similar load. 'Values' are considered essential to the definition of social work, and they are also seen as its sole base or one of its indispensable bases. They are also considered to be a source for the technique of social work, an explanation of the motivation of certain people to enter the occupation and also of particular aspects of the interaction of social workers and their clients. In brief, 'values' are placed at every strategic point in the structure of social work.[1]

Values assigned to different parts of the structure of social work

(a) Values and the meaning of social work

Lindeman (1949) envisaged social work as science at work in the interest of human values: 'what takes place between the social worker and the citizen constitutes a moral equation'. More recently Vigilante (1974) gave social work values a similar central importance when he referred to them in terms of actuality as 'the fulcrum of practice, as permeating decision making and as fundamental in the development of the theory with respect to service provision from the perspective of both direct service and social policy and planning'. It is one of the central arguments of this book that values have a persuasive quality in relation to a practice, but also that this quality can only be grasped when 'values' are treated in a less than wholesale manner. Others see social work as explicitly standing for a number of preferences, though it remains unclear how these preferences cohere into some kind of connected set or system, if indeed they do, and how the preferences are justified. So, Pernall (in Kendall (ed.) 1970) claims of social workers, in ringing tones:

> We value life, we value man's humanity to man, we value respect for man, we value the true dignity that comes to the giver as well as the recipient of respect. We value the gifts that come with the abundant life, but only if these can be shared. We value the 'good' society that permits these things to be.

She then adds a sentence that turns these banner-raising 'values' into necessary requirements for the continued existence of social work: 'If these are not the values we hold and for which we earnestly work, then we shall perish.'

There are problems with the last formulation, of course. It shares with many other statements of social work values a kind of inflationary euphoria: the mode is almost exclusively in the key of idealism. What is lost, if we say simply 'We respect man' instead of 'We value respect for man', which at least directs attention at one set of attitudes and actions (respecting) rather than two (valuing and respecting)? However, the statement is relatively straightforward – we know we are in the cheering game – and it does refer at least by implication to possibly conflictual areas (we, as social workers, value gifts *only* if they can be shared). The possibility of conflict between or within values is more usually avoided. A good example of avoidance can be found in Siporin's illustration of the idea of 'both-and' values from a number of apparent cases of having one's cake and eating it. He suggests that social workers value both independence *and* interdependence, 'openness and probity in self-expression, tolerance and the setting of needed limits, self-awareness and empathy, self-help and mutual aid, competition and sharing co-operation . . . good manners and genuineness' (1975, p. 73).

He goes on to state that 'To hold such values in common often requires their reconciliation and the finding of some balance between them.'[2] He quotes with approval Aptekar's argument that the value that symbolises professional social work is that of balance. Yet talk of 'balance', of 'reconciliation', and of 'both-and' values systematically distracts attention from the necessity of choice in the realisation of what is most valued in any particular situation.

It might be considered that values are central to the meaning of other professions besides social work, but it is often argued that values hold a special significance for social workers. Levy's study of social work ethics (1976) encapsulates the move from social workers as members of a profession to social workers as moral idealists:

> Social work is a value-based profession. It is not only a way of doing something, but a constellation of preferences concerning what merits doing and how it should be done. It is suffused with idealistic aspirations for people and idealistic notions about how people should be treated . . . practices and concerns that are not expected of ordinary mortals are expected of them [social workers]' (p. 238)

It is as if social workers existed not so much, to quote Gwendoline in *The Importance of Being Earnest*, in 'an age of ideals', but somehow in a precipitate of them. Yet some account has to be given of ideals and of morality in social work, even though these are often unhelpfully treated as inextricably interwoven within the seamless concept 'values'.

(b) The value base

In social work, 'values' are sometimes pictured as simple and permanent preferences held aloft for all to see (as in the above quotation from Pernall), but at other times the metaphor of base is used. It has become quite common to refer to the value base of social work either on its own or in company with another, different kind of base, that of knowledge. So, Gordon (1965) remarked what he considered a significant change in thinking about social work, 'A shift in emphasis to finding social work in the value-knowledge realm rather than in the *function* or *activity* or *method* realm'. He believed that this move presented 'The major hope of social work's surviving as a profession in an increasingly science-oriented culture'. Yet, as we shall see in Chapter 7, distinctions between knowledge and value are not easily described and justified, and it is not always clear how social work actively springs from a value (or, come to that, a knowledge) *base*. Two illustrations may help to clarify these two criticisms, even though the questions raised are large ones, requiring further consideration.

First, the distinction between 'value' and knowledge has been considered by Bartlett (1970), who raises questions concerning the status of such statements as 'there is interdependence between individuals in this society' which figure in accounts of social work values. Is this, she asks, to be counted as a value, as in the original American Working Definition (see Chapter 4), or as a demonstrable fact? She goes on to argue that statements identical in form can be interpreted as part of knowledge or as an expression of value. 'The idea that home is the best place for a child is an example: it can be taken as preferred or as a hypothesis for investigation.' Her solution to the difficulty so framed leads us into further complications: 'it is the *intention* regarding the proposition, rather than its actual substance, that makes the difference' (p. 63). More work on the actual forms of the substantive propositions may solve the problem without recourse to the complex notion of intention. For example, the statement 'there is interdependence between individuals' could be analysed in terms of mutual dependence between individuals for certain services, for certain social functions and so on (factual statements capable of refutation), and in terms of mutuality that is recognised by the author of the statement as the kind of mutuality that ought to be.

The second illustration of the problem of discerning the connections between 'base' and activity comes from a study of the operationalisation of one of the most frequently mentioned social work values, self-determination (Kossal and Kane, 1980). The study found

> great variability in the way practitioners interpret and apply the concept of self-determination in specific situations. The variability is even more striking because the sample was limited to one community that is fairly homogeneous philosophically, and most respondents were graduates of a single school of social work . . . our respondents were able to justify very different courses of action as complying with self-determination. When asked for a definition of the concept, however, the respondents tended to be very similar in reciting the standard definition of self-determination and its traditional limitations.

Too much should not be made of a small study, but it does raise questions concerning the relationship between 'base' and activity when one element in the value base (self-determination) is given the same definition and this apparently leads to *very* different courses of action *as* complying with that element.

(c) Values and techniques

Values have been seen not so much as solemn preferences for which social workers stand, but as the source from which social work techniques might be derived. Thus, the Social Work Task (BASW, 1977) speaks of 'skills derived from values', but does not indicate the manner of derivation. Bernstein (1970) in a discussion of group work argues for the 'development of both methodology and values' on the grounds that 'unless values are identified, assessed and implemented, the enterprise is flying blind. Values give it sight, vision and discernment. Values without *implementing* methods would be just as unfortunate' (italics added). Values and methods are, he suggests, interactive, but this seems in his treatment simply reducible to the proposition that clients and workers may learn from each other: 'values are components of the dynamics of the interactions'.

The worker presumably has struggled with choices and has

arrived at some decisions. The agency, the profession and the community play their parts. The worker must insist on some standards of behaviour, and he should feel free to share with the group what he thinks and believes, trying not to alienate those members who disagree. A main goal is to help members learn to think about values. As they work on them, they may well come up with insights which a receptive worker finds helpful. He should be ready to learn from the members. The decisions about which values to accept must be made by the members. The contributions of the worker help to make such decisions better informed, more rational and more humane.

It should not be assumed that 'values' somehow operate only at levels far removed from considerations of practice, but as the two quotations, from the Social Work Task and from Bernstein, suggest, the relationship between 'values' and the techniques of social work is not at all clear.

(d) Values and social workers

'Values' may be seen, as by Bernstein, as giving social work both vision and close discernment, but it is also argued that social workers enter and remain in social work because they can thereby achieve certain valued objectives for themselves. Thus, Holme and Maizels (1978) argue that the motivation for entry into social work is distinctive: 'as an occupation [it] represents for the individuals concerned an attempt to find a way by which they more easily experience themselves as human beings . . . [and] find some form of self-realisation' (p. 47). This apparent myopia finds an echo in Auden's criticism of the conceit of social workers: 'Writers can be guilty of every kind of human conceit but one, the conceit of the social worker: 'We are all here on earth to help others; what on earth the others are here for, I don't know'[2] (*The Dyer's Hand and Other Essays*, Faber, 1963, p. 14). This is not a particularly coherent criticism, since 'helping' is simply not understandable outside certain ideas which embrace human objectives (helping people to realise particular valued states) and certain descriptions (helping people as neighbours, as parents, as social workers), and these descriptions are part of action and reaction. However, reference to the values that social workers may seek to realise through their own social work does enable us to recognise useful distinctions drawn by Downie and Telfer (1980) between the 'aims of the caring professions as embodying values'. They distinguish the *intrinsic aims* of the occupation, that is, the aims which a social worker has *as* a social worker, the *personal aims* of particular workers which might have been pursued in another occupation, and the *extrinsic* aims 'which a particular worker may pursue as a *result* of being a member of his profession but which go beyond it' (p. 10).

(e) 'Values' in the study of consumer opinion

The systematic study of the beliefs and perceptions of the consumers of social work services is a relatively new development, but it is already clear that, for some investigators at least, a consideration of values figures in the explanation of the findings. Thus, Sainsbury (1973) states: 'The comments of several clients related to ethical or moral value, and it proved difficult to separate their regard for moral and ethical aspects of helping from their regard for material and emotional help.' Their relationship to such value appears complex, however, and somewhat elusive of grasp, encompassing apparently 'identification with the value-orientations of their social workers' (p. 3), the weight clients gave to ethical considerations (p. 103), and their appreciation of 'the ethical and emotional goodness' of the social worker (p. 104). These descriptions are not necessarily incompatible, but their compressed use helps us to see only generally that different kinds of appreciation may be at issue.

A similar difficulty arises in the study by Rees (1978) into the interactions of social workers and clients. The complexity of the influence of 'value judgments about people' (moral, judgments, presumably) and of other judgments, some of which involve moral and non-moral values, is well brought out in the following passage, in which the author attempts to penetrate to the centre of the decisions made by social workers in his study:

> Case outcomes were affected by the interplay between practical contingencies and the processual and conditional nature of value judgments which were the hub of decisions. In some cases the social workers and their clients were explicit about their moral calculations. In other cases these criteria were not so easy to discern because of attention given to other topics. For example,

social workers stressed some other constraints which affected their performance of their job: technical ones (e.g. their knowledge of resources); professional ones (e.g. their assumptions about appropriate roles for trained staff); extra-organisational ones (e.g. the pressure from other agencies). The social worker's use of value judgments were intertwined with these other considerations and difficult to disentangle from them.

Disentanglement is not, however, mainly a matter for empirical investigation: social workers make judgments about the attention 'other topics' rightfully command, they distinguish between pressures at least in terms of legitimacy, and so on. In other words, it is difficult to know what is the hub of a decision, that around which it revolves, and difficult to see precisely the special way in which it is moral. It is also difficult from the account Rees offers to be clear what social workers are doing with 'values': they are making judgments which *amount* to moral evaluations (more or less?); they are using a value judgment as a basis for a decision, or value judgments ultimately *affect* the decision, for example, on whether or how to intervene; values (together with beliefs) play an important part in a social worker's general *ideology*.

A quotation from another part of Rees's book will help to illustrate some of the complexity of this last position, which fashionably treats 'values' as the equivalent of ideology. Rees thinks of an ideology simply as an interconnected set of ideas. Several sets can apparently be identified, but he concentrates on the set to which most social workers subscribed, because it 'supported their beliefs about the attainment of some ideal state of affairs in the future'. This general ideology 'manifested beliefs and values which enabled them to make sense of their work'. Sense-making involved 'explaining to themselves and others a reason for choosing their job'; it involved adjustment to the implication that they had some responsibility in relation to almost any conceivable difficulty; 'it also involved responding to society's dilemma about the value and meaning of help and the desirability of employing professional social workers to provide it' (p. 42). Now, what is not at issue is the possibility that the beliefs and the values (two distinguishable elements, as we shall see) cohere in some way, though the coherence is not easily established. What is at issue is the ambiguous nature of 'ideology' in Rees's argument: does the general ideology of social work happen to make sense of the work of social workers and does it make *good* sense? Does it so fall out that an ideology happens to enable various 'explanations' to be given and presumably be accepted by oneself *and* by others (two rather different considerations), or is the set of ideas judged to be an ideology or an effective ideology to the extent that such explanations are considered satisfactory? These questions (and others such as those concerning the distinction somewhat clouded by Rees between 'worthy character', 'worthy decision', and 'worthwhile helping') are raised not through any pedantic obsession about definition as such (Plamenatz once correctly observed that most people understand each other more easily than they understand each other's definitions). They are raised because the functions of values and the kinds of value involved in social work, those of workers, managers and clients, appear to be much more complex than the lists of espoused social work values or simple reference to 'ideology' suggest. In this complexity we need to examine statements about values in some detail so that we may attend to any clues to be derived from different formulations in the same author or within the general work on the topic.

'Values' in social work writing

Having seen the different locations at which 'values' are considered to operate in social work we shall now consider the main ways in which the subject of 'values' has been characteristically treated. Writing on 'values' in social work can be loosely characterised as falling into three main groupings: accounts of social work in which rather generalised references to 'value' or 'values' appear; essays or collections of essays in which some critical assessment of social work values or a particular value is attempted; and work of a more empirical character which is concerned to study social work values in a direct manner. Whichever grouping is considered it cannot be argued that in social work 'values' have been satisfactorily or very thoroughly considered. It is worth enquiring why, since the answers to such a question help us to see how value questions are characteristically treated and how values are viewed in social work.

First, social workers and social work students do not appear to press for *systematic* study. Pumphrey noted in a volume on the curriculum study in America that

> Value teaching seemed (to students) a thing apart from performance. . . . For example, 'respect for the dignity of each individual' was commonly affirmed but students expressed bewilderment as to how one showed 'respect'. When one teacher related the instrumental value of 'confidentiality of disclosures made in the professional relationship' to 'respect' a lively class discussion followed (1959, p. 40).

Second, and related to this, there is 'general vagueness as to the exact kind of value behaviour required in social work practice'. Such vagueness, of course, may be built into the confused idea of 'value behaviour': value behaviour is not a special kind of behaviour, but behaviour in response to certain requirements. Third, it is assumed that whatever social work values are, students are already sufficiently familiar with them. So Bloom (1975) refrained from discussing 'the traditional social work values of individuality, self-determination and the like, because . . . there is little need to convince persons who have selected themselves for advanced training in the helping professions to learn to accept these values; they already hold them' (p. 143). Others assume that the values of social work are simply those of American or Western Society, and such values are already very well known. Such an assumption has been critically formulated by Pumphrey (1959) as follows:

> *Social work values are not in any way distinctive* from those any good person in our North American culture would hold. While social agencies want their staff to be value conscious and ethical on their jobs, this is largely provided for by the process of growing up in a democratic society such as that to which professional entrants have long been exposed. (p. 16)

This book argues against exclusivity in the treatment of 'social work values', but to place them in the general cultural atmosphere is to run the risk of losing touch with them altogether.

(a) Generalised references

Generalised references to 'values' have become increasingly frequent in books on social work. Gordon Hamilton's previously much-used text (1940) on the theory and practice of social casework has very few explicit references to 'values': the single reference to 'value judgment' states:

> Social workers cannot and should not be impartial in the face of individual and social misery and evil. The place of value judgments is always assumed, but they do not take the conventional form of praising or blaming the person who is to be helped. (p. 40)

Quite what form they take is left unclear in this very brief treatment, which seems more taken up with what would now be considered as a distinct question, namely helping 'workers to understand their own impulses to save or to punish, to indulge or to deprive' (*ibid*). (Incidentally, saving, punishing, indulging and depriving are much too complex to be satisfactorily considered as objects of impulse. Can anyone be said to entertain an impulse to *punish*, for instance?) More characteristic of the recent treatment is the collection of readings entitled *Social Work and Social Values* (Younghusband, 1967). The contents of this work include, besides articles on ethics and social work and the assumptions underlying social casework, articles on ego-deficiency in delinquents, communication with the patient, understanding and evaluating a foster family and so on. The list of contents suggests, in other words, that 'values', whether cultural or ethical, seemingly of no consequence, are simply 'everywhere' in social work practice. The reader is given the task of identifying which 'values' are being exemplified and discovering how they are being discussed. With no guidance and no helpful principle of discernment it is not possible to say how the collection has been constituted and hence how helpful it is *as* a collection.

(b) Critical essays

More critical comment on the concept and use of 'values' in social work is found in single essays, like that by Pearson (1975), or collections, such as McDermott's (1975) selection of social work and philosophical writing on self-determination and aspects of liberty. These essays mark a constructive response to Levy's criticism (1973) of

> the tendency in social work literature to list routinely and indiscriminately a series of so-called social work values as if nothing more need to be said for all to understand. The complexity of some of the items far from affirms this, but social workers who talk with one another and write for one another are prone to assume that these value items are self-explanatory. They are so accustomed to citing these items, almost by rote, that no explanation seems necessary – and certainly not for one another. This may be one of the reasons for the limited progress in coping with professional value issues.

Yet it remains unclear in Levy's criticism how far values are seen as 'a basis for guidance and evaluation in social work practice' or as 'root premises of social work', and how far they are to be treated as preferences or as commitments. This latter distinction is of particular importance.

A similar kind of comment can be made on other, more vigorous criticisms of the way social work values are usually treated. Statham (1978), for example, correctly observes that discussion of values in social work is often parochial, abstract and lacking in any feeling for historical context, but this is surely the fault of the discussants whose grasp of the varied uses of 'value' leaves something to be desired. Statham's own hold on 'values' appears at least at times to be unsteady. What meaning can be given to her statement that 'values may in a limited sense have an independent existence' (p. 21)? Is it not simply arbitrary to say that 'philosophy . . . begins and ends at an abstract level and the nearer it comes to the situations in which social workers are involved the more irrelevant it becomes'? (p. 23–4). Similarly, Pearson's robust reversal of traditional social work value seems to be based on the simple assumption that the explicit value orientation of social work can be understood only as 'a set of subsidiary statements which issue from the core *sentiment* of individuation' *or* as a 'prescriptive code relating to client–worker transactions' *or* as a 'disguised system of technical rules for effecting change in client behaviour' (italics added). The values, as a simple list, are not readily comprehensible, but problems of differentiation and of the discussion of relevance for particular circumstances indicate that they are best seen as summary statements of a multi-functional kind. Social workers may interpret social work values in a more *simpliste* manner, but the complexity should not be lost.

(c) Empirical studies

Empirical studies of social work values are not numerous. They range from the positivistic application of a Social Values Test (McLeod and Meyer, 1967) to more open-ended, qualitative studies of an observational (Latimer, 1978) or questionnaire kind (Channon, 1974). Latimer's innocent question at the conclusion of her study, which avoided 'attempts to define what is meant by the value component' is applicable to all the empirical studies: 'Should we and could we with profit now attempt to explore the concept of "values" in a theoretical sense before embarking on further field study?' In other words, such empirical work as has been attempted (praiseworthy in its attempts to connect more closely 'value' and action) is premature in so far as its grasp on 'value' is hesitant and clumsy. Let me try to illustrate this criticism from two of the empirical studies, Channon, and McLeod and Meyer.

Channon (1974) sees the necessity of escaping from the study of that list of social work values that has somehow or other gained recognition in the literature, and achieves a set of over a hundred 'values' held by the social workers in the study. These are divided in terms of work, clients, clerical staff, other staff in the hospital, the hospital, the social work profession, and the community. Yet whilst it is stated that the social workers hold these values, it is left unexplained what it is to 'hold' the value of, say, 'authority', of 'clients', of 'variety', of 'good working conditions' and so on. Does a social worker appreciate 'good working conditions' with just the same emphasis or value or interpretation as he or she appreciates loyalty in colleagues, or friendship, or maturity in clerical staff? More importantly, Channon seems not to appreciate the significance of justification in talk of values: to say X and Y hold the 'same' value, but seek to justify it in different ways, suggests an incomplete notion of value. Channon reports that

> Where the same value was held by more than one social worker within one of the relationships, observations suggested that this 'value' had somewhat different behavioural and motivational

connotations for each social worker. For example,
'co-operation' was a shared value in relationship with other staff
at the hospital. However, the reasons given for engaging in
co-operative behaviour varied considerably i.e. the behavioural
expression of co-operation was influenced by the worker's
thoughts about co-operation –

> 'Others expect you to co-operate';
> 'If you don't co-operate with others you cannot expect their
> co-operation';
> 'I think we have a definite responsibility to co-operate';
> 'I value co-operation';
> 'In an organisation like this you have to co-operate to get
> things done'.

These comments, with the exception of the simple statement 'I
value co-operation', indicate the fruitfulness of asking respondents
to do more than list or state their values, but the full implications
have not been grasped. The reasons are part of the 'value', and to
say that the respondents share the 'same' value but for very different reasons obscures an important part of the meaning of 'value'.
'Co-operation' is a different activity according to whether one is
engaging in co-operative activities for their own sake ('I value
co-operation' can be so interpreted) or because of feared consequences, for valued objectives of the organisation ('You have to
co-operate to get things done') or of one's own social work ('If you
don't co-operate with others you cannot expect their co-
operation').

Channon was attempting to avoid simply discovering that when
social workers were questioned about their values they replied in
the spirit and the terminology of the 'official' training establishment
list (self-determination, acceptance, confidentiality and so on),
McLeod and Meyer (1967) make no such attempt, but abstract ten
major value dimensions from the literature, whilst admitting that
'Some of these are more primary or central than others. Some are
more concerned with existential questions of what is than with
questions of what should be. Taken together they represent an
attempt to reduce to minimum elements that might be termed the
philosophy of social work in the broadcast sense.' The ten dimensions are as follows, with the first-mentioned pole as the value
position towards which the author believes social workers tend:

individual worth versus system goals; personal liberty versus societal control; group responsibility versus individual responsibility; security-satisfaction versus struggle; relativism-pragmatism versus absolutism-sacredness; innovation-change versus traditionalism; diversity versus homogeneity; cultural determinism versus inherent human nature; interdependence versus individual autonomy; individualisation versus stereotyping. Respondents were given ten attitude statements in relation to each of the ten dimensions and were asked to indicate degrees of agreement or disagreement with each statement on a four-point scale. The use of dimensions rather than position acknowledges some of the complexity of 'value', and it is of interest that amongst the trained social workers and those in training there are quite large numbers of low-scorers in all dimensions, and in the case of diversity, relativism-pragmatism, personal liberty and innovation-change there are slightly more low scorers than high amongst those trained. (High scorers are those whose answers are in the direction assumed to represent the dominant social work positions.) This suggests considerable differences between social workers, though the authors are more interested in comparisons between the three groups of trained, in-training, and untrained.

It is not easy to avoid the judgment that more conceptual preparation would have produced a better result. The Social Values Test is basically about public espousal: those statements made in a 'test' situation that can or ought to be made, irrespective of constraints of any kind. It does not attend to the problem of conflict between values. When values can be proclaimed one by one, the respondent is under no obligation to state what value one places upon them. More conceptual curiosity would have enabled the authors to exploit this use of 'dimension'. They seem to be unsure whether they are polarising views that are contradictory or conflicting, or contrasting, and each of these words describes a very different logical relationship. Some of the polarities, they suggest, encapsulate views that are viewed as both 'legitimate or acceptable to some degree by social work'. Other dimensions are more in the nature of beliefs than values. For example, in relation to security-satisfaction vs struggle the authors state, 'Another basic value in social work is the *belief* that individuals must have security, acceptance, and satisfaction of basic biological and culturally acquired needs in order to develop their maximum potential' (italics added).

Conclusion

Chapter 1 indicated that the general importance of social work values was widely acknowledged, though not always explicitly, and was recognised by proponents of different approaches to social work. Chapter 2 has demonstrated the different points at which social work values have been located and the failure of the litera- ture, by and large, systematically to consider the implications of the different kinds of work value-talk was supposed to do in social work and to explore these distinguishable elements hidden under the global sign 'values'. These last two criticisms can be further illus- trated from two previously unremarked features of value-talk in social work.

First, it is always worth attending to the varied verbs connected to 'values' or, more graphically, the kinds of things we are supposed to do with them. So, Pumphrey (1959) speaks of 'affirming', 'apply- ing', 'using', 'teaching', 'selecting', 'stressing', 'possessing', 'not isolating', and 'adhering to', values. Similarly, the Central Council for Education and Training in Social Work report on values (1976) speaks of 'value judgments', 'value difficulty', 'value questions', 'value commitments', 'value positions', 'value difficulty', 'value emphasis', 'value preference', 'value contradictions', 'value dilemma' and so on. Now, the point is not to suggest that each of these (and other) terms indicates an important distinction or that there is necessarily any inconsistency. It is to draw attention to these features of our actual discussion of values and to suggest that we are given clues to what 'values' mean in the many different activities we use 'value' to accomplish: we make special kinds of judgment; we appear to raise special questions (of value and not of fact); we state particular difficulties, or affirm a commitment to certain beliefs or outline a position; we seem to affect the behaviour of others through the transmission of values or their imposition. Attending to the many different tasks we seem to give to 'value' may help us to move beyond an understanding of social work values other than that rather minimal grasp that suffices for fight or for celebration.

Second, the expression 'values' is frequently coupled with other words which tend to widen the scope of meaning very considerably. So it is by no means uncommon for 'values' to be closely linked with 'attitudes and principles', with 'attitudes' or 'expectations' or with attitudes and a code of ethics'. Despite this widening of embrace, 'values' in social work are invariably but implicitly treated restrictively as moral, without any specification of what constitutes morality.

'Value' appears frequently in social work literature, but value-talk is undeveloped, and conversation about values or social work values has hardly started. This is mainly because it is assumed that everyone knows what values (or beliefs, or ethics, or philosophy, or attitudes or preferences) are; that a value is a value, is a value; and that values may be elaborated but cannot be argued about. It seems to be agreed that values play a crucial part in the practice and definition of social work, but 'values' are connected to social work practice in many different ways. The concluding argument of this chapter is that social work values require sharper analysis before they can be truly celebrated, and that the literature on values in social work offers many avenues for deeper exploration. How can such work be advanced?

The problem can perhaps be summarised in the following way: the social work literature does not treat with sufficient imagination and rigour the problems posed in the conceptualisation and in the placing of social work values, but this should not lead to a discarding of what people have written. Rather, we should just attend more closely and critically to the literature and also to the problems of the social worker making choices. For these reasons the next chapter considers one aspect of the making of moral decisions, namely making a conscientious choice, whilst Chapter 4 re-examines some of the more usually cited values and some neglected disvalues to increase understanding of their implications. Later chapters will seek to widen the context in which social work values are discussed by considering historical aspects and the conceptual treatment of values outside social work. The objective of the historical and conceptual work is illumination rather than regulation, and this chapter will have failed if the reader is not by now convinced of the existence of shadowy areas in the treatment so far accorded to social work values and values in social work!

3

Conscience in social work: towards the practice of moral judgment

'His conscience is such an elastic member,' Hilary pointed out.
'It seems to permit things outside the usual range. I don't
suppose it will turn fastidious for our convenience.'
    'It may require a little guidance,' Honeychurch said.
E. Candy, Bones of Contention

'You know, Brevda when you come to think about it, life is hell.'
    'It notoriously has its negative aspects, sir.'
    'There seems no rest from having to decide what one ought to
do in a given situation.'
    'The necessity of moral choice can be most onerous, sir.'
    'Self-interest just isn't a sufficient guide to behaviour, is it?'
    'Sadly deficient in many respects, sir.'
    'After all, there is such a thing as right and wrong.'
    'Bravely spoken, sir.'
Kingsley Amis, Russian Hide and Seek

Introduction

Social work values and values in social work cannot be exhaustively
treated in any single volume. The present work should be seen as a
preliminary mapping of the terrain and as an outline of certain ways
of making progress in crossing it. This chapter takes as its starting
point the individual practitioner faced with a consideration of one
inescapable question: 'What ought I, or the client, to do in a particular situation, from a moral point of view?' A consideration of

conscience in social work will help us to come to terms with some important aspects of this question. It is not thereby assumed that everything important about values in social work can be reduced to issues of conscience, or even that moral values in social work can be reduced simply to matters of conscience. One of the central problems in the whole discussion of values in social work is that the same term – for example 'good', to select one from a range of value-words – applied to a piece of social work activity can mean different things: technically good, in so far as the 'correct' rules of professional practice were 'invoked' and applied; aesthetically good, because the actual form of the social work on that occasion evoked or would evoke the admiration of professional peers (as in a 'beautifully handled' interview, irrespective almost of outcome); morally good, since particular moral objectives were reached or morally admirable relationships were created or sustained. Beginning with conscience does not seek to blur such distinctions, nor does it assume that conscience is king in a united realm of values. Yet it does more than simply refer to the source and the resolution of moral problems. It can be taken as representing certain important aspects of the whole problem of values in social work. How can it succeed in this respect?

First, considerations of conscience highlight the individual and the social aspects of decision-making in social work. The idea of the 'individual' social worker is criticised because it abstracts the individual from the collective, but logically there is no escaping the fact that judgments in conscience can only be made by the individual in relation to the individual's own action. I may reach the view that your action is immoral; I can only make a judgment in conscience of my own action. This does not mean that such judgments are idiosyncratic psychological reactions. As we shall see, they remain judgments. Nor does it mean that these individual judgments are reached somehow on one's own or in isolation, deliberate and necessary. It does mean that the idea of a *social* conscience – however fruitful in the work of sociologists such as Durkheim – should be treated very critically in considering the actual decisions in conscience of individuals. Conscience, of course, 'belongs' to the activity of humans, and it is not only social workers who are faced with the necessity of conscientious decisions.

Second, 'conscience', as we have perhaps already come to appreciate, is not a simple notion. It requires conceptual analysis before we can begin to be clear concerning its meaning and implications. In this way it can stand for the whole range of terms in value discourse, each of which requires analysis.

Third, considering 'conscience' in social work is not a kind of ivory (church) tower activity; it usefully connects social work considerations to those involved in ordinary conversation. Such normal usage presents problems and also a challenge. 'Conscience' is invoked by unobtrusive scoundrels as a quiet justification for treason, or by public figures advertising their desire for the contradiction of a nicely judged political martyrdom, or by 'the kind of conscientious objector who believes that he has no obligations except those he has thought out for himself' (Emmet, 1958, p. 40). It also serves to defend considerations of conscience in social work against a charge of preciousness or of over-high moral seriousness. St Thomas More is an example of the ordinary working of conscience and also of the conscientious objector as most reluctant hero.

Fourth, discussion of 'conscience' connects the study of social work with projects in understanding and action far wider than social work itself. 'Conscience' has been systematically considered at great length by a large number of philosophers and theologians, and the nature of conscience has been very variously interpreted. Some twenty years ago Wand (1961) very usefully summarised the range of views:

> It has been said . . . that it is fallible (Broad), that it is infallible (Butler); that it's ultimate (Rashdall); that it is the voice of God (Hartman), or the voice of custom (Paulsen); that it is merely advisory (Nowell-Smith), that it is a command internally imposed (Mayo); that it is conscious (Butler), that it is unconscious (Freud); that it is a faculty (Butler); that it is not (any contemporary moral philosopher); that it is the disposition to have certain beliefs, emotions, and convictions which, when operative, issue in conscientious actions (Broad) and that it *is* conscientious action.

Even this list can be extended, since it is not only contemporary moral philosophers who criticise the idea of conscience as a faculty. Aquinas, for example stated:

> Strictly speaking, conscience is not a faculty, but an activity, namely the actual application of moral science to conduct.
> (*Summa Theologica*, LXXIX, 13)

I mention this particular view not simply to lengthen an already impressive list, but rather to underline a distinction which is of some contemporary importance. The notion of conscience as an activity seems helpful in considering the place of conscience in social work.

But how has 'conscience' figured in discussion of social work so far? It appears in social work in a number of distinguishable propositions: it is a synonym, for the practical purposes of social work, for 'super-ego'; it justifies, in its collective form, the institution of social work and the entrance of some or all neophytes into the profession; it explains, again in its collective form, the changing face of social work and social provision in general. These forms of usage need clarification before a hold on conscience and the social worker can be secured.

Conscience and super-ego

In expositions of Freud's threefold categorisation of personality functions (and particularly perhaps on social work courses) it is not uncommon to hear 'super-ego' treated as the equivalent of 'conscience'. This is incorrect even within Freudian theory, since the relationship between super-ego and ego-ideal and the contrast between them are the subject of debate.[1] Such discussion is not irrelevant to the major concerns of this chapter in view of Cupitt's assertion in a Christian context that 'Conscience is the voice of my ego-ideal' (Dunstan (ed.), 1975). Even this is not a very helpful identification if we accept Freud's description of the ego-ideal as the expression of admiration the child feels for his parents as idealised objects. The more important point, however, concerns the ways in which 'conscience' is not the equivalent or even the rough equivalent of the super-ego.

A Freudian view of the super-ego precisely disregards moral feelings or those experiences of shame, guilt and remorse that 'belong' to having a bad conscience in relation to what one has done or failed to do, and those experiences of being at peace with oneself which 'belong' to having a good conscience. The super-ego, in Freudian theory, does not register moral feelings, but feelings evoked by some threat to security, feelings of anxiety, fear and dread rather than remorse. As Jones (1966) has argued, the phenomenon of a bad conscience is not constituted by objectless anxiety or dread. A person is said to have a bad moral conscience because of certain beliefs he consciously entertains about himself. Feelings that are moral (shame, guilt, etc.) are appropriate – in the case of a bad conscience – only when a person has failed to do what he *believed* to be right, and not when he has unconsciously complied with unconscious threats. Now the crucial significance of moral intuition and moral beliefs in any consideration of conscience is an important point – 'conscience' is more than a matter of 'having' feelings, more than 'having' feelings that are describable as moral. 'Conscience' refers to moral feelings *and* to reflection and decision on what one ought to do in a particular situation. Failure to grasp the concept of conscience surely accounts for the surprising absence of any reference to conscientious behaviour and judgments of conscience in situations seemingly demanding just such reference. In relation to counselling and social work in abortion, for example, 'conscience' is rarely mentioned, though careful attention is paid to emotional reactions, feelings of emotional comfort or discomfort, and so on.[2] Such feelings are important, no doubt, but they have to do with conscience only if they are moral feelings.

A Freudian view of the super-ego treated as synonymous with conscience also prevents our grasping the development of conscientious judgments as human persons move through their biographies, and suggests that such judgments stem ultimately from too simplified and too unified a source. Rieff (1965, pp. 273-4) describes these shortcomings of the Freudian view in the following manner:

> It is precisely the religious view of conscience as intelligent and reflective as well as passionate that here comes under attack, for Freud argues that conscience is furnished by social authority and remains, unreflectively, at authority's disposal. This refusal to acknowledge that conscience may be at odds with its social sources surely simplified the moral process. Because he views society reductively, as the family-in-large, Freud overestimates the degree of consistency in the ethical influences to which people are exposed.

This comment supplies a helpful corrective to the tendency to treat super-ego and its development as the same subject as the development of conscience. It also indicates the notion of conscience developed in relation to intelligence and reflection as well as to passionate conviction. Conscientious judgments are conceptually connected to a person's own behaviour, but the reflection and the origin of the material from which the judgments are made derive from social sources in a wide sense. The person making a conscientious judgment may not thereby be in good company but he or she certainly operates within a human context.

Social conscience

For social workers, though perhaps less for students of social policy, the idea of social conscience is used as a positive answer to a number of questions, some of which at least have moral import. Sociologists, on the other hand, may view 'the social conscience' as a kind of determining force, whilst some philosophers have been critical of the very notion. Kolnai (1977), for instance, believed the idea was 'diseased' because it hindered or prevented the taking of a genuine interest in objects and problems *as such*. To take such an interest, argued Kolnai, requires at least a phase of complete indifference to any 'welfare' or service interest as such, whether private or social. In social welfare, however, 'social conscience' has been viewed neither as a disordered notion nor as descriptive of a constraint. The notion has been used in two main ways: to justify social work and to explain the development of legislation and social provision. Each use calls attention to an important set of questions, and both distract attention from the idea of conscience. It is important to see how this is done.

The relationship between the occupation of social work and 'social conscience' has been stated most clearly perhaps in a book by Towle (1954). Her approach is made up of a number of propositions, though any differences remain unremarked by the author: *Social work should attend, or cannot help attending, to the development of social conscience.*

> Social work, by its very nature and function and because of the group it serves, as well as the nature of its relationships with its supporting public, must give great emphasis to the development of a high degree of social conscience and social consciousness. (p. 13)

Social work attracts people seeking solutions to problems of conscience.

> Social work by its nature, in that it rather literally is taken to

represent the conscience of the community, in that it is literally thought of as playing a parental role in the lives of people, draws some individuals who need, through identification to support their own superimposed consciences. (p. 79)

Social conscience has led to the occupation of social work.

Social work exists because the community has had a conscience about the disadvantaged and an altruistic impulse to protect those who need help for survival. This conscience seemingly is a compound of many elements, several of which are discernible. First, man's propensity to feel with man, so that, as he comprehends himself in the position of the disadvantaged, he is impelled to succour them out of feelings of self-injury and guilt. When the numbers of the disadvantaged grow great, they comprise a group that threatens the peace of mind and heart of those who otherwise could be comfortable. Second, around the core of man's necessity for identification, he has developed, as he has experienced satisfying and constructive family and other group life, a feeling of obligation to others and a capacity to care for others. (pp. 13–14)

However, it seems that though conscience is seen as a compound of anxiety in the face of threat, of identification with the disadvantaged and of a feeling of obligation, the social worker should not identify with the fears of the community. Towle noted that it was possible in terms of 'a highly developed social conscience' to see the social worker as a member of a minority group. 'This is because much of social conscience lies dormant, unconscious, potential, whereas the expressed conscious conscientious attitudes and motivations of the social worker often represent a minority' (p. 15). The 'community's conscience is a vital force to be awakened for use', though the activity of the social worker 'may precipitate a threatening awareness which often is resisted, so that frequently the community conscience can be put to use only gradually' (p. 15).

The treatment of 'social conscience' and, almost incidentally, of 'conscience' in these passages exacts a heavy toll from these concepts. 'Social conscience' in particular seems to be required to do too much work. It is called on to justify the institution of social work; in the description of what attracts new recruits; as a tool of social work; as featuring in the overall objectives of social work.

'Conscience' is not distinguished from 'consciousness': the possibility of an 'unconscious' conscience is left undeveloped (arguably because the Freudian 'super-ego' informs the basis of the whole approach), and 'conscience' is used unhelpfully as shorthand for a range of attitudes, fears, emotions, and judgments, few of which appear to be moral. In brief, whilst the social roots and ground of social work are undoubtedly important, treatment of *the conscience* that is social indicates problems rather than solutions. A similar omnibus view of 'social conscience' can be found in the study of social policy when criticism is mounted against what has come to be termed the 'social conscience hypothesis'[3] concerning the development of social legislation and provision. In the 'social conscience' perspective changes in social legislation and social provision are explained either in terms of the state of the social conscience or in terms of developments in the social conscience. Criticism of this viewpoint is justified, though it tends to ignore the elements of moral evaluation and judgments in the development of social provision, collects too many notions into the single term 'social conscience' and uses 'conscience' as a synonym for a more or less explicit programme of action, motivated by a range of notions of what is desirable, what is *possible* and what is to be most feared in the social situation.

'Conscience' more fully understood

To rescue 'conscience' from some of the distortions of welfare we can begin by considering ordinary use and usage. We speak of someone 'acting from conscience' and someone 'acting conscientiously' or 'being conscientious'. The first seems to describe a special situation, almost a heroic one, in which someone has his back, so to speak, against the moral wall; the second suggests plodding attention to duty almost for the *sake* of moral routine. Undoubtedly, our consideration is more frequently directed to 'conscience' on the heroic scale. So conscience has been conceived as a command issued by the Self to Self; Shakespeare in *The Tempest* spoke of conscience as 'this deity in my bosom'; whilst Pius XII in a radio broadcast in March 1952 called conscience 'the innermost and most secret nucleus in man . . . [where] he takes refuge with his spiritual faculties in absolute solitude'. Yet it is misleading to think of 'conscience' as being applicable only to the rare situation of a St Thomas More or a Hamlet, or as implying that every moral situation has to be seen afresh and responded to anew and entirely in ways thought up for oneself and by oneself.

'Conscience' is best seen in terms of content (the *critical* consideration of what a person ought to do from a moral point of view) and of function (the doing or the attempting to do that action which he ought to do). 'Being conscientious' is by no means the whole of morality, but it is a necessary part of being moral – ('Since we cannot be saints we need to be conscientious' (Garnett, 1969) – and the purpose of moral consideration is not a state of *being* (conscientious) but some action. So, 'in appealing to conscience, a person *by that very appeal*, is committing himself to act morally' (*ibid*.). Moreover, what a person's conscientious conviction indicates in relation to action binds with a rather special authority. The most frequently quoted illustration of the kind of authority envisaged comes, of course, from the work of Bishop Butler:

> Thus that principle, by which we survey, and either approve or disapprove our own heart, temper and actions, is not only to be considered as what is in its turn to have some influence . . . but likewise as being superior; as from its very nature manifestly claiming superiority over all others: in so much that you cannot form a notion of this faculty, conscience, without taking in judgment, direction, superintendency. . . . Had it strength as it had right: had it power, as it had manifest authority, it would absolutely govern the world. (Sermon II)

Butler correctly describes the three components of the idea of conscience – judgment, direction (i.e. towards action) and superintendency – but his rousing hymn to conscientious imperialism requires some qualification. Conscience binds the individual, but it is only in special circumstances that even a person's rights of conscience are acknowledged, and we cannot decide in conscience what another should do and certainly cannot rule others through our conscience. Because someone has decided something in conscience we are not thereby obliged to help him so to act or to refrain from any interference in his action. This is not only because others have consciences or, as Broad (1969) says, 'What is sauce for the conscientious goose is sauce for the conscientious ganders who are his neighbours or his governors'. It is also because when we refer to someone's right to follow his conscience 'we mean that he does no wrong to proceed on his honest convictions, even though we disagree with these convictions, and even though, for policy or other reasons, we must force him to act contrary to them' (Dworkin, 1979, p. 189).

Conscience and the social worker

I have tried so far to build up a picture of 'conscience' through criticism of current usage of the term in social work and social welfare and through brief reference to some general questions concerning the status, meaning and authority of conscience. It is in these ways that we shall be able more fully to grasp the idea, even though what has been offered is a sketch of some possibilities. Suppose, though, that we could now or later get a better hold on 'conscience', what use would this be to the practising social worker? I would emphasise two important considerations.

First, a recognition of the importance of conscience highlights the inescapability in human affairs of the question 'What ought I to do in my situation?' This is not to say that every client of a social service or every social worker ought to become, or ought to be helped to become, a kind of moral worry-guts. Yet there are situations facing clients and social workers in which the question 'What ought I do from a moral viewpoint?' (rather than a technical or prudential or an aesthetic point of view) is insistent. Silber (1969), for instance, in a careful study of moral responsibility in various different cases of illegitimate birth, has drawn our attention to the neglected question of responsibility for what we *are* or have become (his term is 'status responsibility') even when there is no bond created by intention or negligence connecting what we are with what we have done. Whether or not this element of responsibility is recognised, the essential point is that no amount of indoctrination, no politico-social programme, can make the moral decision, as it were, on our behalf or, somehow, without us. Even with a programme and a theory as all-encompassing as that of Marx, there remains a gap between theory and practice. Wicker (1976) has noted its significance in relation to moral decision. He accepts that the question, what should he do, cannot be answered until he is satisfied concerning the basic nature of the society in which he lives. 'But even when I have done that, for example, by concluding that the basic truth about my society is that it is governed by a fundamental contradiction between the forces and the relations of production within it, I am still far from knowing what, in practice, I ought to do about it.' He appears to offer two reasons for this, though I find the second more convincing: there is insufficient detailed consensus amongst those who accept the analysis; less contingently, 'it is in the nature of the case impossible to translate that theory into any detailed programme for individual choice. For such is not the purpose of the theory. . . . In other words, I am faced with a choice that I have to make precisely because of the very gap between 'foundation' and 'superstructure' which allows Marxist analysis to occur at all.'

Second, even though conscience decisions cannot, and should not, always prevail as far as outcome is concerned, social workers ought to respect conscience and work at, and help others to work at, its formation. There will, of course, sometimes be a conflict between the conscience of the professional and that of the client, but we may assume this to be the case more frequently than we need. In other words social workers should attend with care to what Catholic moral theology terms the issue of co-operation, i.e. those questions which arise when a person is asked to co-operate in the act of another. Curran (1975) has recently argued for a revision of the limits of co-operation on the basis of new teaching on religious freedom. He cites as an illustration the case of the doctor who believes in his own conscience that sterilisation for contraceptive purposes is wrong, but has a patient who believes it is morally and medically good: 'Here is a conflict of rights – the rights of both to follow their own conscience.' However, Curran suggests that the doctor could operate 'without co-operating with the bad will of the patient because the patient has no bad will in this case. . . . In this society we daily live with people who do things we believe are wrong. Without unduly sacrificing his own conscientious principles, the doctor could argue that in this case he is providing the service for which this individual person has a right. . . . The doctor by his action is not saying that this particular operation is right.' Such a view, argues Curran, does not justify any type of co-operation, since one should not co-operate with another if this harms the rights of innocent persons or the peace and common morality of society. Curran's discussion sheds some light on a stubborn problem which requires much more study, but it is at the cost of importing into the discussion such difficult notions as the undue sacrifice of conscientious principle and the peace of a society.

Conclusion

Considerations of conscience do not exhaust the subject of morality and are but one part of the subject – more extensive than that of morality – of values in social work. However, developing the preliminary treatment given in this chapter may constitute a helpful beginning for social workers not only in the consideration of moral problems but also in studying the more general type of values in social work. 'Conscience' refers to more than feelings; it is concerned with the development of commitment to particular ideas. To place a special emphasis on 'conscience' is not to argue that a person ought to do unquestioningly what he or she has been taught to do or that a person should do what he or she believes he ought to do; it is rather to emphasise the activity of critical consideration of what one ought to do *and* of acting on the resulting conviction. 'Conscience', as we have seen, concerns an individual's consideration of his or her own actions in the light of what is right and wrong, but properly understood it is not the lone activity of an isolate. It may be true, as Norman (1971) has argued, that the line between 'conscience' and 'moral egoism' is hard to define. However, Norman's criticism that the idea of moral integrity *by itself* gives no content to the ethical life leads to the view that moral integrity involves fidelity to a moral ideal. So a rounded view of conscience[4] cannot be separated from ideals nor, I now add, from some of the other major components of value-talk to be identified in later chapters.

4

Traditional values and neglected disvalues

Acceptance can be shown in other ways than accepting assault, and acceptance is of value only if it is honest; I see no reason why it may not be qualified: 'I accept and respect you but not your alsation or the attention of your baby to my handbag.'

M. Crompton (1980), p. 182

It is all to easy to write ourselves as social workers out of the script in the name of client self-determination only to take up the director's role.

M.Simpkin (1979), p. 3

The social worker has at times, as we have just seen, to make individual judgments about what he or she ought to do in a particular situation from a moral point of view. Social workers have to form judgments and make decisions about the kinds of situations they should strive to realise, as worthwhile, from a range of situations all valued, and about the methods to be used to attain ends considered to be 'good' – from a technical, aesthetic, moral, prudential, etc., point of view. To help with judgments and decisions of these different kinds 'lists' of social work values have been compiled from time to time. The purpose of this chapter is to reconsider these lists and some of their most important content in order to reassess the 'values' usually cited in the social work literature, and to consider the neglected issue of the negative values or disvalues which actively regulate what is considered to be good social work. These disvalues are not simply the reverse side of positive values. For instance, by saying that there is a close connection between social work and 'democratic values', then it may be assumed that social work and fascism are incompatible. To say social work is, in some sense or other, 'democratic' is to say at the same time that it is not fascist. Rather the disvalues I have in mind are those that actively indicate situations that ought positively to be avoided by social workers. So, in this chapter, special attention is given to paternalism, and man-ipulation, as possible instances of disvalues. Whether discussing the usual list of social work values or the disvalues, I shall attempt to consider how these 'values' can presently be best understood and what it means to refer to them as values. In neither case should it be assumed that the treatment is exhaustive.

'Traditional' values reconsidered

(a) The list approach

The following statement could not be considered in any way unusual:

> The ethical values which underlie casework, are:
> (a) To respect the client
> (b) To accept him for himself
> (c) Not to condemn him
> (d) To uphold his right to self-determination
> (e) To respect his confidence
> These all grow out of the ideals embodied in the democratic principles of our western way of life, with its emphasis on the value of each unique individual. (National Institute for Social Work Training, 1964, p. 19)

This listing bears a close relationship to the authoritative discussion by Biestek of the principles of the casework relationship (1961), though Biestek also includes individualisation, the purposeful expression of feelings and controlled emotional involvement. Characteristically, however, discrepancies between lists remain unremarked and hence unresolved. Clues possibly pointing towards a more complete understanding are not taken up. This means that the rather vague idea of a set or system of values is left to perpetuate itself without any close scrutiny as to whether what is listed hangs together in some *form* of coherence. Marxist critics are in this connection of little help, since they simply assume and assert both

that the 'traditional' values of social work are systematically connected and that this cohesion is readily identifiable if not standing
self-confessed as social democratic or welfare capitalist. It is so
identifiable largely on functional grounds: the values are so obviously those required by capitalism. The possibility remains unexplored that the admitted success of the working class in making
successful inroads on capitalism to establish the welfare state could
also have been accompanied by gains in the realm of ideology.

Other critics have attempted to describe the overall value system
of social work, but it is significant that no single description seems
adequate. Take, for example, a recent characterisation by Downie
and Telfer (1980):

> It might be said that what we have discerned in the practice of
> the caring professions is a moral system of the kind which is
> called by philosophers 'ideal utilitarianism'. Ideal utilitarianism
> may be said to have two elements: the principle that right action
> is that which promotes as much good as possible for everyone
> (this corresponds to the value which we called 'philanthropy')
> and the belief that this good is to be seen, partly, no doubt in
> terms of what the people concerned want, but partly also in
> terms of *ideals* which are not simply reducible to what people
> want. (pp. 36–7)

Even this seems problematic, in so far as social work at any rate
seems often to be torn between a rather exclusive concern with
those who turn out to be clients, a broader interest in those who
might be recruited to such a role, and a concern with promotion of
the good of everyone. However, accepting this description of ideal
utilitarianism, it is significant that for Downie and Telfer it is not of
itself sufficient as an account of the underlying moral principles of
the caring professions. The pursuit of the greatest good of the
greatest number is limited by a number of other principles which
cannot be reduced to the former. Amongst these Downie and Telfer
note: respect for persons, the right to life, the right to liberty, and
the right to know the truth.

Taking a list approach towards social work values also tends to
distract attention from particular connections between some at least
of the values concerned: it is as if the list separately identified
distinct items of equal significance, and of identical form.

At least some of the values usually espoused for or by social workers are interconnected, though different kinds of connection can be discerned. Thus, the CCETSW report on values (1976) argues that respect for persons should be understood as an attitude 'which it is morally appropriate to adopt towards persons conceived as self-determining and rule-following beings', Others may agree that the description under which persons are to be respected is crucial, but suggest that persons ought to be respected simply because they are self-determining. However, the point at this stage is that respect and self-determination go very closely together. Similarly, other writers see a logical connection between certain values. So Butrym (1976) states that 'The principle [of individualisation] is logically derived from the uniqueness of individuals', though she leaves unstated and unexplored how anything other than a technical or at best a prudential principle (do this to achieve this result or attend to this aspect if you wish to succeed) can be derived from the admitted and simple fact that there is always some respect in which A is different from B, C, D and so on. Again, the relationship sometimes appears to be neither logical nor that of a more inclusive attitude nor a part of the meaning of the more inclusive principle or value, but one of overlap. This is most apparent in a consideration of two espoused values, usually given entirely separate treatment – acceptance and being non-judgmental. To accept something or to accept a person (two different activities, as we shall see) is incompatible with condemning them, though being non-judgmental (i.e. *refraining* from or avoiding certain 'judging' activities) says nothing about acceptance seen as a positive activity, as a constructive reaching out towards unexpressed aspects of the personality.

(b) Three lists considered

Thinking of the espoused values of social work as 'listed', in a textbook for instance, obscures differences of substantive content and of mode (as 'is' or 'ought' as 'right' or 'needs'). These differences begin to emerge if we compare 'lists'. The following summary of three separate lists of social work values is based upon Teicher's discussion of the American working definition of social work practice, Biestek's fourteen values, and Teicher's own formulation. Teicher's statement that this 'enunciation refutes the notion that all

that exists in this field is ambiguity and confusion' seems to exagger-
ate the extent of agreement. (I have not followed Teicher's order of
presentation in the attempt partly to bring like items together and
partly to point possible contrasts and differences.)

Working definition	Biestek	Teicher
The individual is the primary concern of this society.	The dignity and worth of the human being is supreme.	Each individual has dignity and worth as an individual.
There are human needs common to each person, yet each person is emotionally unique and different from every other.	Man is endowed by nature with potentialities and powers in the physiological, intellectual, emotional, social, aesthetic and spiritual areas.	Each individual ought to receive respect and considerate treatment.
	Man has an innate thrust and obligation towards the realisation of his potentials.	
	Man has a capacity for choice and because of his obligation for self-realisation he has the right of self-determination.	
There is interdependence between individuals in this society.	Each person is an individual, and he has a *right* and a need to be so considered.	Each individual ought to take part in making the decisions that affect him.
They have social responsibility for one another.	Man has the right to the appropriate means for the realisation of his potential.	Each individual ought to be free to develop his own capacity and talent.
An essential attribute of a democratic society is the realisation of the full potential of each individual and the	Each person requires for the harmonious development of his powers socially provided and socially	

Working definition	Biestek	Teicher
assumption of his social responsibility through active participation in society.	safeguarded opportunities for satisfying his basic needs in the physical, psychological, economic, aesthetic and spiritual realms.	
	Man's social functioning is important in his striving toward self-fulfilment.	
Society has a responsibility to provide ways in which obstacles to this self-realisation . . . can be overcome or prevented.	Society has the obligation to facilitate the self-fulfilment of the individual.	
		Each individual ought to share fairly in the control of goods and services.
	Society has the right to enrichment through the contributions of its individual members.	Each individual ought to have full and free access to the information he needs for rational behaviour.

The more these lists are pondered the more uncertain what is being asserted becomes. Some items, for example, appear simply insufficient in both form and content: self-realisation, self-fulfilment as such, without serious and detailed qualification, cannot sensibly be accepted as a goal, and how could the right to *appropriate* means for the realisation of potential be framed in any particular case, and against whom would it be pressed? More generally, these lists confirm the unhelpfulness of treating 'value' and 'values' in an undifferentiated way. The only way in which sufficient sense can be made of these lists is to reinterpret what are variously stated as factual or value statements or as rights or needs or obligations. A need basis for social welfare requires a different justification than one concerned with rights and produces a different set of practices. Some of the statements are better seen as indications of ideals or ideal situations (e.g. 'Each individual ought to share fairly in the control of goods and services'); others are concerned with encouraging human purposive behaviour ('Man has a capacity for choice and because of his obligation for self-realisation he has the right of self-determination'). Still others should be viewed as rules. Again, differences of a significant kind will become apparent if we explore the distinctive grounds for a rule such as individuals should 'have social responsibility for one another'. It is possible to see at least three distinct possibilities. Social responsibility (however defined) may be grounded in the idea of service to others or what Gouldner (1973) has called the norm of beneficence. Action towards others is justified simply because particular others are in need. Alternatively, social responsibility could be seen as arising from the norm of reciprocity (Gouldner): one gives services of different kinds in the generally confident expectation of a broadly equivalent response to one's own predicament over a period of time. Finally, social responsibility *for one another* may be grounded in what Gerard (1982) has called the norm of solidarity, which implies an identity of interests and shared concerns with the deprived.

These general comments on some of the lists so far assembled strongly suggest the extent of further work required before any one item or the elements of coherence can be established. The following section begins to do some of this work in relation to particular values that invariably find their way on to the lists.

(c) Some particular values

In this section, having critically discussed 'the list' approach and some particular lists, I consider some examples from the values usually espoused. The objective is to illustrate the problems involved in trying to grasp their meaning and the difficulties the meaning or range of meanings may create in social work. It is not possible within the present space to attempt an exhaustive treatment of all the commonly asserted values or even of those chosen for relatively detailed discussion. I have attempted to concentrate on the most problematic. None of the usual social work values is without problems, of course. Confidentiality, for example, may have a weak or strong reference: what is treated as confidential may be only what is specifically *confided*, information that is entrusted explicitly or implicitly; or what is so treated may be *any* information gained through carrying out a particular role. There are also problems in relation to access to whatever information is defined, by whatever processes, as confidential; does the client, for instance, have a right of access to 'his' or 'her' confidential file? Confidentiality is not, however, very difficult to define, and the problems it creates in social work seem much less difficult than those involved in acceptance, self-determination, and respect for persons. It seems to function in a relatively straightforward way as a norm or rule, but different reasons for the rule may be advanced. It may be grounded in either a prudential, a technical or a moral judgment. In other words, we ought to treat all or certain information as confidential because people tend to trust those who are experienced as trustworthy (prudential grounds), or because not handling material in this way will create certain problems in social service delivery (technical grounds), or because gossiping or carelessness about someone else's personal information counts as an act of disrespect (moral grounds).

Acceptance
One of the main acknowledged difficulties with this 'principle' concerns practising social work in the light of that 'principle'. Difficulties in distinguishing the elements in 'acceptance' are less openly admitted. An example of the former problem can be taken from the recent CCETSW study (1976), in which acceptance is spoken of as 'Perhaps one of the most difficult of social work principles to put into practice, and one which causes the most painful moral dilemma'. Acceptance was viewed by the study group as being expressed in continuing to value a person because of his inherent worth, irrespective of who or what he is, and as such may be one of the most important ways of conveying respect. They believed that the expression of the principle could sound patronising, but that its aim was 'to help workers stay with clients with whom they find it hard to sympathise or whom they may find repulsive'. This discussion suggests that one of the difficulties in putting the principle into practice may derive from the problem of coherence as a particular 'value'; it moves perhaps too easily into respect and into the avoidance of moral or condemnatory judgments. Difficulties

may also derive from the changing grounds on which it is advocated: as a recognition of the inherent worth or value of the person; or as a technical means for assisting social workers in delivering services on a universalised basis, i.e. not on the basis of selection according to the social worker's strong dislikes or likes – all are equally to be accepted. An earlier discussion illustrates further problems concerning what 'acceptance' is and what reliance on acceptance rules out. Davison (1965) calls 'acceptance' an attitude rather than a technique; 'it is constant no matter how unacceptable [the client's] current behaviour may be'; it 'leaves no room for criticism or condemnation; indeed it implies that the worker renounces the role of judge' (p. 9). This treatment raises a number of questions, though the notion of a 'value' as ruling out certain behaviour or attitudes is generally useful. However, if 'acceptance' is a social work 'value', does this rule as inadmissible any judgments in terms of unacceptability by the social worker? In other words, has Davison simply omitted quotation marks around 'no matter how "unacceptable" ' and thus not stressed the difference between what is unacceptable socially and what the social worker finds unacceptable? Alternatively, it could be envisaged that social workers form judgments partly at least on the basis of unacceptability, like other people, but these are overridden in some way or not directly expressed. Certainly, the close connection between the roles of judge and critic unhelpfully blocks any discussion of the function of criticism in social work and of the possible roles of praise and blame.

A way through these and other problems with 'acceptance' is to make a number of distinctions. Acceptance as an attitude should be distinguished from a range of actions intended to achieve certain goals. The objects of acceptance should be distinguished (e.g. the person, or the person's actions as having a point from his perspective, or the 'deeper' significance or the causative factor leading to these actions or the formation of his particular personality). Finally, the social worker should attend to the different descriptions under which the acceptable is accepted. This last reference to what people or their characterisations are accepted *as* or the spirit in which they are accepted can be illustrated by a quotation from George Eliot's *Adam Bede*: 'These fellow-mortals, everyone, must be accepted as they are: you can neither straighten their noses, nor brighten their wit, nor rectify their disposition.' This suggests that people should be accepted under the main description 'unchangeable', but it also points to the manner in which this acceptance is best expressed, i.e. expressed in a way appropriate to *fellow-mortals*.

As a conclusion to this consideration of acceptance in social work I would suggest that acceptance should be seen as more than an attitude. It refers to actions that can be described as accepting acts, but such acts are only fully appreciated *as* accepting when they have achieved their purpose. These acts involve refraining from such other actions as expressing rejection, condemnation, totally negative criticism, but they are not constituted in and by such restraint. It is persons or the characteristics of persons that are the objects of acceptance, and persons are accepted not because they can be only what they are (i.e. we would like to change them if only we had the effective means) but because this is one of the appropriate ways in which people should be treated under the description 'persons'. Acceptance is one of the values held by social workers in so far as it takes the form of a rule against certain behaviour. The rule can be justified on technical grounds but could also be seen as grounded in a view of human behaviour valued as purposive: acceptance is directed at the point of a person's behaviour despite any appearances to the contrary.

Self-determination
A brief comment in *The Essential Social Worker* (Davies, 1981) suggests that this value – the longest established, as it were, in the social work firmament – has recently been exposed as something of a fraud: 'Both Plant and Whittington, effectively killed off the concept [of client self-determination], but the idea has remained a powerful fiction in the minds of practitioners' (p. 64). Concepts, particularly complex ones, are not so easily disposed of, however, though the difficulties in grasping and applying self-determination are such that announcements of its demise may be counted as wish-fulfilment.

> The right to freedom, to self-determination, is one of the most difficult of human values to comprehend. It contains so many variables that descriptions and definitions are precarious and hardly ever satisfying. . . . It appears to be an ever-changing concept, affected by innumerable contemporaneous happenings in the culture in which it is found.

So wrote the authors of the only attempt to trace the history of the idea of self-determination over fifty years of social work writing (Biestek and Gehrig, 1978, p. 4.). Certainly, it has been evaluated in different ways by social work writers. For Perlman (in McDermott (ed.), 1975) self-determination is nine-tenths illusion but one of the grand illusions. Aptekar (1955) sees it as possible the single concept without which modern casework would not exist. Biestek and Gehrig (1978) argue that self-determination is 'the first logical consequence and test of the supreme value' (of personal worth) (p. 4); that it is essential to the implementation and conception of that supreme value (p. 4); that self-determination is necessarily implied in all the values of social work (p. 5). Bernstein (in McDermott (ed.), 1975) values self-determination as a citizen rather than the king of a realm of social work values. These distinct valuations placed on the same concept, the apparently changing nature of the concept, and the determined attempts to reveal its sham or illusory force, suggest at least the possibility that 'the same concept' means very different things to different writers, as, in Chapter 2, we noted that practitioners can use this same term to justify different courses of action.

The term proves, in fact, to be quite elusive. It may refer to helping people to attain what they want, and only what they expressly want, because it is what they want. It may encompass action only on those decisions that are reached through a particular kind of decision-making process (i.e. a process that produces enduring, serious commitments to particular actions). Finally, the term may characterise the whole process of social work whereby people develop their power of self-direction. However, some clarification can be achieved if we use some distinctions, particularly the idea of a social work value as expressing rules of behaviour or ideals or valuations. So, it is useful to ask what sorts of behaviour are ruled out and what ruled in as valued by someone who, in a social work context, espouses the value of self-determination. Biestek and Gehrig (1978, p. 32) have suggested how social workers in America in the decade before the Second World War might have replied to such a question:

What caseworkers should not do
Persuade.
Directly change a client's attitude and behaviour or manipulate them.

Do things for or to the client.
Control and direct the client.
Advise: offer plans unsolicited.
Assume responsibility for the case.
Pre-determine the conclusion.
Give approval or disapproval.

What caseworkers should do
Be psychologically active to understand the client and outwardly
    passive to help the client act freely.
Introduce stimuli (such as an educational process) which will acti-
    vate the client's own resources.
Create a relationship environment in which the client can grow.
Give perspective to a client's problems.
Offer suggestions without pressure.
Help clients move at their own pace.

It is not necessary to accept either these significant 'do's' and
'don'ts' or the author's view that these statements 'indicate some
noticeable *progress* from the preceding decade' (italics added) in
order to see that asking what behaviour self-determination rules in
and rules out constitutes a useful question. Probably in contemporary social work we would wish to rule in under 'self-determination'
at least a generally participative mode of working and to rule out at
least coercion,[1] though not rational persuasion, and interference
save in essential matters of health and life/death, though not
rational influence. We would also question some of the rules of an
earlier age (for example, some responsibility for a case is surely
assumed in the offer of social work) and the extent to which, though
they may lead to desirable behaviour, they should be seen under the
description 'self-determination'. In this way, we can increase our
grip on 'self-determination' in contemporary social work.

A hold on the notion of self-determination can also be streng-
thened by considering 'self-determination' as an ideal, as client
freedom commendable in itself or leading to valued conditions or
qualities. In discussions of client self-determination it does sometimes seem that the most important consideration is some ideal of
the human condition which should be approximated as far as possible. So, an ideal is entertained of the human being as fully self-
determined, fully self-responsible, fully self-helping. When writers

stress the place of reality in the modification of self-determination they are, implicitly or explicitly, treating self-determination in an ideal manner. This can usefully be contrasted with discussions of self-determination which emphasise the role of self-determination in a person's growth to social and emotional maturity or in the development of social responsibility through suffering the consequences of one's own actions. In such a context, self-determination is viewed as valuable in the production of some end result; theoretically it could be compared with other ways of attaining the same end (provided, of course, conditions such as maturity were not defined in terms of self-determination). It is, however, a characteristic of much of the discussion that self-determination is not treated as something valued comparatively: problems of self-determination are usually treated not as a question of valuing on an occasion some other quality or condition (say fraternity) more highly than self-determination, but as a question of a limitation on client self-determination itself. So, Biestek and Gehrig (1978, p. 76), because they see self-determination almost as a necessary and sufficient condition of social work, are unable to consider self-determination as against other 'values'. Instead they qualify:

> Freedom is not synonymous with licence. Freedom is not meant to promote rampant individualism. Freedom is a means not a goal in itself. It is a means for attaining the person's legitimate goals in life. They include the development of his own personality and his relationship to other persons. The basic individual freedom, therefore, does not sanction self-injury or self-destruction in any of these areas.

Respect for persons

In the social work literature 'respect for persons' is sometimes treated as a separate value or principle and sometimes embedded in the idea of the 'supreme' value of the individual. Biestek and Gehrig (1978) illustrate the second usage when they state that the social work profession

> selects as its supreme value the innate dignity and value of the human person. It maintains that nothing in the world is more precious and noble than the person, and that every person is worthy of respect. Social work, of course, is not alone in

subscribing to this value. It is common to many other
professions and to most cultures and societies.

The suggestion that an occupation arrives at its values by selection
rather than recognition of what is involved in a practice is of considerable interest, but more importantly it is arguable that the notion
of comparative valuation as applied to 'persons' is an unnecessary,
even a self-defeating, strategy. Valuing the person in a comparative
sense (selecting as 'most precious', stating that nothing is more
precious than the person) leads to questions concerning that against
which the person is assessed in terms of preciousness and nobility,
whereas the point of the argument is to remove 'person' from
comparative valuation. In an important sense of 'value', 'persons'
refers perhaps uniquely to that on which a value should not be
placed by anyone. Persons should simply be cherished as such. So,
the core element is best simply discussed as 'respect for persons'.
This idea has been fairly extensively discussed in recent philosophical work,[2] and Plant (1970) has indicated in relation to social work
that one of the main problems concerns the place of this 'value' in
social work:

> the three concepts, individualisation, acceptance, and
> self-direction are in fact deductions from the concept of respect
> for persons. They are deductions from this concept in that they
> are a part of its very meaning. Respect for persons is, on this
> view, the basic value in casework. (p. 11)

The place of 'respect' will be considered shortly, but at this point
Plant's treatment can be used to illustrate the general, positive
appreciation of 'respect for persons' in social work. In particular,
Kant's maxim that persons, including oneself, should be treated
always as ends in themselves and never simply as means, receives
frequent favourable mention in social work writing. Recently, however, Kant's formulation, which is not without difficulties of
interpretation, has been criticised by social work writers. Simpkin
(1979), for example, states that 'respect' is 'only too often a cover
for pity and even contempt' (p. 99), and respect for persons 'offers
no positive criterion for action, is open to widespread abuse and
ultimately does little more than provide a spurious moral refutation
for attacks on individualism' (p. 98). Abuses, of course, abound,
but there is no reason to suppose that 'respect for persons' is

characteristically more likely to be abused or abandoned for pity and contempt. It *is* more difficult to see the relationship between 'respect for persons' and action, but less so when the place of that 'value' has been discerned. It is certainly not the case that the Kantian idea is empty of content. It has recently been fruitfully used as part at least of the justification for such different theories as Nozick's view of the minimal state and of the individual life that can only be led separately and Rawls's (1972) emphasis on self-respect (with which respect for others is closely related, psychologically and logically) and the welfare of those least advantaged by any particular social arrangements.

In social work it has been more usual to assert than to analyse 'respect for persons'. This habit tends to reinforce the view that 'respect for persons' is no guide or even illumination. Exploring the place of this 'value' and the meaning of 'respect' and 'person' should help us to see the kind of guidance we can properly expect and the kinds of activity that might count as the showing of respect to persons or the treating of persons with respect.

'Respect for persons' is more like a summary of a way of life or a morality than a single moral principle. It resembles the basis of rules or the reason for helping to achieve human purposes rather than a rule or a purpose. Telling someone to 'go and respect persons' conveys no instruction at all; 'be respectful, whatever else you are' assumes that 'being respectful' consists in a simple and single attitude. Moreover, 'person' and treating people as 'persons' have built into them a complex range of ideas of rationality, dignity, life and so on, and no simple rules can be deduced from them. Nor can 'respect for persons' be satisfactorily viewed as an ideal, so that 'respect' is qualified with regard to reality or people are accorded more or less respect in so far as circumstances permit. On the contrary, 'respect' seems something that *is* owed to persons and a due that belongs to them rather than something to be weighed out and allocated on the basis of more and less.

Yet 'respect for persons', though it is not a rule or an ideal, does have direct reference to action. It extols a range of attitudes, or readiness to act towards people described in morally preferred ways. Now the attitudes have been variously described in the literature, but each one can be legitimately attributed to 'respect', though failure to appreciate the differences may have contributed to the belief that 'respect for persons' offers no positive criterion for action. Downie and Telfer (1969), for example, argue that the attitude in question is one of cherishing:

> to cherish a thing is to care about its essential features – those which, as we say, 'make it what it is' – and to consider important not only that it should continue to exist but also that it should flourish. Hence, to respect a person as an end is to respect him for those features which make him what he is as a person and which, when developed, constitute his flourishing. (p. 15)

Others see respect as an attitude closer to wonder and awe or as preparedness to recognise what, in the liberal tradition, are called the rights that belong to persons, or as readiness to treat people with dignity – notions of 'rights' and 'dignity' being somewhat more distant than cherishing or concern that someone flourishes. Darwall (1977/8) attempts to answer questions arising from the possibility of withdrawal of respect, such as 'Do we not also think that persons can either deserve or fail to deserve our respect?' and 'Is the moralist who claims that all persons are entitled to respect advocating that we give up this idea?' To create an adequate response, Darwall distinguishes between what he calls recognition respect and appraisal respect. The former consists

> in a disposition to weigh appropriately in one's deliberations some feature of the thing in question *and* act accordingly . . . it is just this sort of respect which is said to be owed to all persons. To say that persons as such are entitled to respect is to say that they are entitled to have other persons take seriously and weigh appropriately the fact that they are persons in deliberating about what to do. (italics added)

Appraisal respect, on the other hand, is bestowed on 'persons or features which are held to manifest their excellence as persons or as engaged in some specific pursuit'. Appraisal respect is the positive appraisal itself and refers to no particular behaviour from oneself that is required or made appropriate. Respecting someone's integrity of character or someone as a skilled practitioner of any act does not entail deliberating about him or acting towards him in a particular way.

'Respecting persons' refers to a range of possible attitudes towards people and also to a range of descriptions under which they are potentially so treated. These descriptions also have implications for action. So, Downie and Telfer (1969) pick out as these features of 'person' as a notion which make it worthy of respect, 'self-determination', and 'rule-following'. Others adopt a specifically religious description and speak of respect as being due to people described as made in the image of God. Quinton (1973) has identified five characteristics of 'person': consciousness, capacity for abstract reasoning, will or agency, capacity for moral praise and moral blame, and capacity for personal relations. Each of these may be found in any particular person in a stronger or a weaker form (e.g. 'rationality may be abstract and linguistic or concrete and practical'), and where characteristics are present in their strongest form we speak of a complete person. Whatever the description of 'person' – and acknowledging respect for persons as a value entails using some description – it is clear that any description of *person* does indicate action that attends to and encourages particular characteristics. If someone respects persons and has the responsibility for delivering certain services, 'respect for persons' is more than a banner flapping out of harm's way. Indeed, some commentators are convinced that 'respect for persons' actively promotes discrimination against those who may not count as persons or as being fully persons according to what are agreed to be the narrow criteria of personhood – children, the senile, the severely mentally handicapped. Watson (1980), for example, advocates the adoption of the principle of respect for human beings on the grounds that this offers a wider range of characteristics relevant in the allocation of status and stigma involved in any social morality: 'Our "respect for human beings" might entail valuing the capacity to be emotionally secure, the desire to give and the capacity to receive love and affection, as well as the distinctive endowment of a human being' (p. 61).

Disvalues in social work

This is a large and, as has already been suggested, a neglected subject. By referring to disvalues I wish to more than call attention to the shadows inevitably cast by 'values'; that is to say, reference is not made to the negatives 'contained' in the assertion of positive values. If, as has been argued, 'love' or 'balance' is the most important 'value' in social work, then social workers are logically against 'hate' and 'imbalance'; but there seem to be 'values' that achieve a high degree of unpopularity, as it were, in their own right amongst social workers. For introductory purposes, two such disvalues have been chosen: manipulation and paternalism. The two may, of course, become connected, and each may be 'outlawed' through self-determination. However, they also represent distinguishable situations which social workers might wish to try to avoid in order to be true to their craft.

Manipulation of the environment has been an objective of social work for a long time and part of the claimed armatorium of the social worker, but the manipulation of clients has been explicitly outlawed. Whether the manipulation of others in the interests of or on behalf of the client is similarly eschewed is doubtful. Brager and Specht (1973), for example, argue in relation to community work, that where the client is a person or a group on behalf of whom work is undertaken the ban on manipulation is less obvious than when the client is in a direct service relationship with the social worker. In the former situation, if the worker surrenders the opportunity to manipulate or advises the client or constituent to do so, he or she 'diminishes even further the ability of the disadvantaged to obtain a re-distribution of resources. Thus professional purity may be most costly to the victims of social problems' (p. 286). The authors suggest four criteria by which manoeuvring should be judged: who benefits, the object of the activity, the substance of the issue, and the nature of the act – 'Manipulative behaviour may include truth arranged for effect, withheld information, exaggeration, distortion, or an outright lie' (p. 290). Generally speaking, their treatment tends not to treat manipulation as a disvalue: 'manipulation should be eschewed *except* when it clearly supports another, over-riding, value. The magnitude of the need, the powerlessness of the constituent, and the rules of the game as played by adversaries dictate the conclusion that manipulation is sometimes justified' (p. 288).

However, whether the issue concerns clients or those who are seen as oppressing them, it is crucial to gain a hold on 'manipulation'. Ware (1981) has recently suggested four necessary conditions which should obtain for an alleged instance of manipulation to be one. A may be said to have manipulated B under the following conditions: (1) B's life style, the goods he chooses or the strength of adherence to such choices are different from what they would have been if A had not intervened; (2) A restricts the alternatives that B may choose so that the probability that B will make a particular choice is increased; (3) B has no knowledge of, or does not understand, the ways in which A affects his choices; (4) a moral agent in A's position would normally be held morally responsible for the results of structuring the alternatives facing B. This view of manipulation certainly argues that the avoidance of manipulation is not adequately described as a question merely of retaining professional purity; issues of human agency and moral responsibility are involved. Manipulation on this understanding is ruled out in so far as the direct 'counselling' relationship of social worker and client is concerned. With regard to more overtly political situations we may conclude that manipulation remains morally disagreeable though it may be politically justified. This is no empty comment, nor is it the confirmation of a chasm between 'moral' personal relationships and the 'immoral' political arena. As Williams (1978) has observed, 'only those who are reluctant or disinclined to do the morally disagreeable when it is really necessary have much chance of not doing it when it is not necessary'.

The subject of paternalism is often discussed in relation to the character and intention of laws, but social work intervention also provides the opportunity to examine relationships that have been described as paternalistic or are judged according to their success in avoiding this label. 'Paternalistic' is clearly a rather deviant variation of 'paternal' or 'parental', and it has been advocated at a particular period in the history of social work that, with certain clients, social workers should play an active parental role or behave towards them as a good parent might psychologically be expected to behave. More generally, Towle (1954) has argued, as we have seen, that society expects the institution of social work to carry certain parental roles. How, if at all, can such suggestions escape the adverse criticism of paternalism (or presumably maternalism, but we are dealing with the terms so far used in a debate that, as far as state action is concerned, has a very long history), and on what grounds is the change of being paternalistic a sound criticism?

The concept of paternalism has recently been fairly extensively discussed, and there seems to be agreement on its general character. Paternalism involves some kind of interference with or inhibition of another's liberty; a turning of someone away from his current preferences or judgments; and the use of a particular kind of justification, generally along the lines that the intervention was in the other's interests or actually furthered his welfare. So Dworkin

(1979) states: 'By paternalism I shall understand roughly the interference with a person's liberty of action justified by reasons referring exclusively to the welfare, good, happiness, needs, interests or values of the person being corrected.' Gort and Culver (1976) adopt a similar approach, though they stress that an essential feature of paternalistic behaviour is the violation of moral rules, such as those prohibiting deception, the deprivation of freedom and so on. This seems to enlarge the category of moral infringement unnecessarily, but their approach generally accords with that of others. They argue that A is acting towards S if, and only if, A's behaviour correctly indicates that A believes the following: (1) A's action is for S's good; (2) A is qualified to act on S's behalf; (3) A's action involves violating a moral rule or doing what will so require with regard to S; (4) A is justified in acting on S's behalf independently of S's past, present or immediately forthcoming (free, informed) consent; (5) S believes, perhaps falsely, that he, S, generally knows what is for his own good.

If we accept these criteria, it does seem that paternalistic behaviour presents some problems for the social worker. These are increased if we examine more closely the question of auspice which, so to speak, authorises such behaviour. Thus, Husak (1981) argues that a paternalistic relationship is necessarily built on a relationship of inferiority–superiority. 'Hence a lack of rationality, prudence, foresight, intelligence, maturity, or some other deficiency or shortcoming in which the alleged inferiority consists seems necessary before paternalistic treatment could be thought appropriate.' It is debatable whether all these possible shortcomings can equally be seen within the single category of 'inferiority', but certainly most recent treatments of 'paternalism' are concerned to establish safeguards around paternalistic treatment or to discuss the grounds on which it might be justified, despite the apparently forceful warnings of John Stuart Mill.

Thus, Weale (1978) suggests three criteria against which paternalistic intervention should be evaluated: the interference with a person's own freely chosen life plan should not be severe; the intervention should be justified by reference to some element in that plan; there is evidently some failure of reason on the subject's part which results in an inability to determine his or her own ends. Dworkin (1979) is concerned with exploring situations in which it is plausible to suppose that fully rational individuals would agree to paternalistic restrictions placed upon them, and he also hinges the reasons for their agreement on the idea of the individual as a decision-maker within some kind of life-scheme. He believes that paternalism can be justified when a person neglects to act in accordance with his actual preferences and desires or as a kind of insurance policy against making decisions which are far-reaching, potentially dangerous and irreversible, or in situations involving dangers insufficiently understood or appreciated. These, and other arguments, suggest that paternalism may not be entirely the disvalue in social work that it initially appears. However, paternalistic treatment, even in conditions of lack of foresight, maturity and so on, should not, in social work, be or become a treatment of people regarded as objects. The fact that it is conceivable to treat oneself paternalistically (Husak, 1981) indicates the central role of a principle long regarded as important in social work, namely that of reciprocity. In view of our perception of social work as a morally serious enterprise, it is perhaps not surprising that some have argued that the principle of morality is the principle expressing the notion of reciprocity.

> Reciprocity is the recognition of the other participants in a transaction as entities having ends and rational ends. That recognition is not just a formality, a brief concession preceding the working out of the elements itself. The recognition of this quality – I shall call it human personality, or personality – must be part of the structure of the end itself. (Fried, 1970, p. 52)

Perhaps the disvalues of social work are best seen and summarised as all those qualities and conditions which prevent social action being characterised as fully human activity directed at human betterment.

5
Three controversies

Conflict of goods is the heart of our problems. Love clashes with honour, order with freedom, art with Friendship, justice with prudence, kindness with honesty – and not just in the rare, melodramatic cases of major decisions, but in the constant, quiet grind of everyday living. Somehow we manage to balance their claims by bargain, compromise, sublimation, partial combination, and sacrifice.

Mary Midgley (1978), pp. 190-1

Unfortunately the moral and intellectual cost of calling a draw a synthesis has been high. When ideas or values are in conflict, and when they negate each other, both honesty and prudence dictate that we do not bury their differences but learn to live with them and try to make their very incompatibilities a source of creativity.

Paul Halmos (1978), p. 68

Introduction

The aim of this chapter is to argue the fruitfulness for the study of social work values of a historical approach which focuses on controversies, and to offer a brief description of some of the main arguments in three major controversies in social work. The main purpose is to point to the illumination to be obtained from the study of these – and other controversies – of two crucial aspects of social work values: their form and their substantive content. Situations in which social workers or at least a significant majority of them have been engaged in more or less systematic argument with each other – and sometimes with those 'outside' social work joining in – have not been common in the history of social work. This is surprising in view of the potential for argument in the critical function of social work and of the range of contestable concepts which imbue social work and mark out the possible boundaries of its activity. Amongst the reasons for the comparative lack of controversy would be the thrust towards resolving potential conflicts in terms of 'balance', a tendency to deal in terms of compromises, a strong desire to maintain at least the appearance of professional unity, and to avoid living with the idea and reality of value conflict between or 'within' people.

Yet on at least three occasions in the last hundred years significant controversy undoubtedly erupted: positions were taken, different viewpoints were expanded and espoused, claims for possession of the truth about social work were confidently made, and passions were roused in a normally quiet occupation. Controversies arose in the course of the debate between the Charity Organisation Society and its critics, friendly and otherwise, towards the end of the nineteenth century; in the struggle between the American schools of social work in the middle of the present century, between the 'dissident' minority of the Functionalists (Keith-Lucas, 1957, p. 124) and the majority Diagnostic School; and the beginnings of controversy can be discerned in the contemporary concern in Britain and America about the meaning, feasibility and justification of a social work practice that is radical.

In discussing these three controversies the intention is not to offer anything like a full historical account, nor to give a historical explanation of the origin and course of each controversy in terms of the biography of the main contestants or the evolution and pursuit of material and social class interests. Enquiries of these kinds are undoubtedly important, and they require careful and detailed work, as contrasted, for example, with unelaborated assertions of the prime significance of social class in the explanation of changes in opinion and view. The work of Stedman Jones (1971) in relation to certain aspects of the activities of the Charity Organisation Society is a notable example of the kind of critical historical enquiry required. Where such detailed historical work has been undertaken the results have been used in the present chapter, but my main consideration is not a full historical explanation. Rather this chapter is more narrowly focused upon the arguments and the questions raised with a view to illuminating 'value' in social work. Can the controversies be helpfully understood as a basic clash of values and, if so, 'values' in what sense and of what kinds? What light do the controversies shed on the distinguishable elements in social work values, on the distinct positions social workers wished to defend, and the causes they wished to advance? Such are the limited objectives of this chapter, but it is worth noting the potential for developing an understanding of social work from the study of controversies. Just as the study of public scandals is a useful source for the study of the development of social policy, so public 'professional' disagreements on basic issues will increase our grasp of what social work is and was, and particularly of its continuity and discontinuity. The already noted assumption that social work is essentially a unitary phenomenon and that it is connected through a direct and simple inheritance with what social work *was* can be tested through a study of controversies.

1 THE CHARITY ORGANISATION SOCIETY AND 'THE SOCIALISTS'

'Charity organisation' appears, at least initially, a somewhat strange notion. As Hobson (1909) remarked at the start of his critical essay on the social philosophy of the Charity Organisation Society, 'It must have occurred to many to ask what the writer of the 13th Chapter of The First Epistle to the Corinthians would have thought of charity that was "organised" '. It is also a notion that has seldom done much to inspire any investigator. The philosopher T. H. Green, whose ideas exercised an influence on the Charity Organisation Society, was constrained to admit that charity organisation was one of 'the two questions of our time which compete with each other in a reputation for dullness' (quoted Richter, 1964, p. 337). Even interest in the controversial position the COS came to take or at least to be identified with on a number of public questions is blunted by the easy assumption that the only truth about the COS is that it was wrong. The opponents of the COS have succeeded in persuading posterity, as they persuaded their contemporaries, that Beatrice Webb can indeed, to use the words of William Smart, 'do all the idealism'. Nonetheless, the Charity Organisation occupies an important place in the development of ideas and the practice of charity: it is no accident that supporters and, as we have just seen, critics use a long historical perspective when reviewing the work. The COS was at its height one of the most important of later Victorian philanthropic bodies, and the controversy between the most influential COS leaders, such as the philosopher Bernard Bosanquet and the General Secretary, C.S. Loch, and those who considered themselves to be more socialist in thought marks a significant debate in the development of thought and practice in social work. Of the three controversies considered it was probably the least confined to domestic social work circles.

The history of the COS has already been studied in broad outline (Mowat, 1961: Roof, 1972: Woodroofe, 1962; Young and Ashton, 1956) and more detailed and critical work has been undertaken (Woodard, 1961; Stedman Jones, 1971). Our understanding of the roles and practice of the COS is still far from complete, and the aim of this chapter is not to retell or to attempt to complete the history of the COS. Our main concern is with the running fight, from approximately 1890 to 1915, between the COS and its critics, both those who described themselves as 'candid friends' and those who found their wrathful candour incompatible with any friendship. This kind of qualification has a general importance in the study of controversy in social work in so far as it directs attention to the possibility of a range of relatively distinct positions rather than a single simple divide. So, in the case of the controversy presently studied, it is misleading to imagine a single-minded and unified COS caught in a Somme-like engagement with the confronting army of Socialists. It is likely that the distinctive groupings within the COS (to which Stedman Jones has directed our attention for an earlier period in the society's history) persisted, and in any case criticism of the society's main stance against state provision and of its untroubled self-confidence in the principles of charity were at the time of the controversy voiced within the society. Thus, the *Charity Organisation Review* (January 1890) recorded a strong difference of view in the Council of the COS concerning a letter from C. S. Loch on the subject of the danger of School Boards feeding children in want of food. Allen Graham stated that

It appeared to him that the Society was in danger of dropping into a position of hostility to popular sentiment, and of alienating some of its oldest supporters. . . . No doubt the doctrine laid down in that letter would be applicable in a healthy and ideal state of society, but the mistake was to assume that society was in a healthy condition. The patient was sick, and the doctrinaires proposed to treat him as if he were well. (*Charity Organisation Review*, January, 1890, Report of Council Proceedings)

Such criticisms, arising from the day-to-day work, should be placed alongside 'set piece' papers from candid friends read to Council by such well-disposed critics as Samuel Barnett (1895) and J. Gamble (1901).

It is also worth noting that the controversy was probably of active interest to a minority of enthusiasts – and this again points to a feature common to the controversies as they were experienced at any particular time. C. S. Loch described this phenomenon in a paper he wrote for the COS Council in 1877:

a friend and critic of the Society once set me thinking, by saying abruptly: 'It is all very well for you to read and study. But you know the members of your Committees don't. They plod along with their cases; but you are quite wrong, if you think they are troubling themselves about general causes, principles, or any other questions.'

Loch recorded that he made no reply. Then as now, what is of urgent or main interest in the relevant literature is important, but it cannot be used as a simple reflection of patterns of behaviour. Moreover, the fact that many practitioners and their managers can or are constrained to practise without explicit reference to controversy and conceptual complexity is potentially of considerable interest in any appraisal of the role of theory in social work.

The argument

The positions maintained on either side and the background of assumptions from which each side selectively drew were complex. Substantively, the arguments revolved around moral value and moral judgment in social welfare considered in a context of citizenship. Formally, what came into disputation were the rules of practice, their status and the extent to which they should be adapted to changing times. Whether considering substantive issues or questions concerning how the distinguishable elements within what are classed simply as 'values' are to be differentiated, this controversy has relevance for the systematic study of social work values.

The disvalue of dependence

The COS leadership believed that systematic reliance or dependence on sources of aid and maintenance outside the family did significant individual and social harm. Those who could with justification be described as social dependants were hardly citizens. This was not because, as has often been assumed, the leadership of the COS believed in some doctrine of abstract individualism; the connections between people were not conceived as being of the kind that could, morally or in other ways, support the long-term dependence or non-selfhood of any significant group in the community. A characteristic passage from C. S. Loch (1909) illustrates the importance of self-sufficiency and sets the idea in a context of social philosophy and social analysis. Society is

> a state of social obligation, the completeness and reality of which is indicated by discriminated and efficient use of function and by individual character, considered as, at bottom, a sense of obligation which is itself co-related to function. But further than this. If the fulfilment of function by a member of society, by a party to the solidarity, is incomplete and faulty, there is a disruption alike in the common organisation of society and in the common obligation. There is a delinquent party to the contract . . . those who fall out of obligation, who can maintain themselves no longer . . . become *ipso facto* not members but dependents.

In similar vein Bosanquet (1909) identified failure of self-maintenance as a defect of a particular and significant kind: it was a 'defect in the citizen character', and as such posed essentially moral problems.

The critics of the COS leadership were also motivated by moral concerns, but of a utilitarian kind which centred more on the attainment of states of social improvement than on any notion of a human life considered as a whole. Their morality was of a more down-to-earth kind than the abstruse theorising of the COS. This can be seen, for example, in the respective ways in which the institution of property was treated. The critics emphasised the responsibilities of property owners to others, and were sceptical of any justification of the institution. The COS stressed the place of property in an individual's total scheme and the role it should play in the project of his life. Bosanquet, for example, argued that the idea of property was an ethical one and that the institution of property enabled people to realise a unity in their lives. Property was an ethical idea consisting

> in the conception of individual (properly speaking, household) life as a unity in respect to its dealings with the material instruments of living. It is not merely the idea of provision for the future; still less the certainty of satisfying wants as they arise from day to day. It is the idea that all dealings with the material conditions of life form part of a connected system, in which our conceptions and our abilities express themselves. It binds together the necessary care for food and clothing with ideas of making the most of our life and of the lives dependent on us. (1951, pp. 281–2)

Now, Hobson (1909), in his criticism of the COS, largely accepted that property could function this way but asked a simple question in relation to 'goods' that arrived as if by magic and certainly without effort by the recipient:

> Are there no other forms of private property which should stand in the dock with 'doles' to the poor? How about gifts and bequests to the rich? . . . Why do the Charity Organisation Society and their philosophers constantly denounce small gifts to the poor, and hold their peace about large gifts to the rich?

Again:

> They are all fear lest the poor should suffer from the degradation and the ignominy of receiving something they have not earned. Yet they never lift their voices to save the characters of the well-to-do which are constantly assailed by these same demoralising forces.

This argument was not lost on Bosanquet – the two sides of the controversy, it is important to note, usually understood each other – though his solution was not effective. He acknowledged that property might demoralise but, unlike long-term dependence on the state, only in certain circumstances; when it could be said to distract from one social vocation, without forming the basis of another. This does not meet Hobson's argument that doles and property are, in COS theorising, treated differently. Doles are judged in terms of their origin; their most important distinguishing feature is that they have not been earned. Property, on the other hand, is judged in accordance with the use to which it is put. The COS, in other words, were vulnerable to the charge of producing one theory for the propertied and another for those without permanent possessions of their own. The COS leadership did not develop strong arguments against this criticism. Instead they dealt with it through a firm statement on the rights and duties of a common citizenship and on the importance of social class unity with a view to achieving social progress through the recognition of a single set of ideals and principles. They believed in the unitary nature of social welfare guided by unchangeable laws and expressed in the primacy given to one particular role. This was usually that of citizen – Loch agreed with the Webbs that medieval ideas of welfare were simply mistaken, and argued for a revival of the ancient Greek ideas of citizenship – but sometimes the notion of unity as in a church was mooted.

The COS also differed from their critics in their sterner view of individual duty and their insistence on the actual moral agency of 'character'. Their critics emphasised social responsibility in relation to the creation of bad or poor social conditions and also to the response that should meet these conditions. Their stance was in marked contrast to any emphasis on individual duty alone, as, for example, in Loch's insistence that charity which fulfils the natural duties of others is in the main wrong and deceptive charity. Charity which helps others to do their duty was in Loch's view the most genuine and salutary as it was the most difficult. The COS certainly emphasised the moral supremacy of the 'able-charactered' person (Holman, 1912). As Bosanquet (1916) stated: 'the principle underlying our work is that we value mind above body; that we value character and intelligence above comfort and external regulation'. The critics argued that this emphasis neglected the role of environmental pressures. 'Is it not likely', asked Mrs Townshend (1911), that the child bred in cleanly habits will wish to be clean, and, in general, is not the way to raise the standard of living to accustom the young to higher ways of life? Even if it is true that character is the most important element in social reform it is equally true that habit is the most important element in the formation of character, and habits of life are conditioned by environment.

Other critics were not quite so confident. Hobson seemed to waver in his criticism of this aspect of COS belief. On the one hand, he considered it to be a half-truth, 'a recognition of the inter-dependence and interaction of individual character and social character as expressed in social environment'. On the other hand, he believed that the resulting emphasis on the priority and primacy of moral reform was a falsehood: 'in dealing with the inert nature of the residuum, direct social support aiming at the improvement of material circumstances will play a larger part'.

For the COS self-maintenance was not an ideal to be approximated, but one within the reach of most if not all men: external hindrance to its realisation was not of decisive importance. The philosopher Sidgwick (1893) expressed the main thrust of COS thinking in a consideration of a concept of importance and influence at the time, namely the notion of a station in life and its consequent duties. Sidgwick acknowledged the importance of external circumstances and then stated:

important as it is to diminish these hindrances, it is no less important for an ethical society to lay stress on the old truth – sometimes apt to be overlooked in our ardent efforts for economic improvement, that it is possible to act rightly under any material conditions.

Mrs Bosanquet considered a more specific question in a welfare context, namely, whether in a situation of housing overcrowding social conditions may not permit people to meet their own responsibilities. Her reply, emphasising the idea of 'trying', was one of the ringing kind:

It is a vain and idle hypothesis. The social conditions *will* permit them; for their very efforts to make them do so will make them steady and efficient workers, whose services will be valued by the community and will be supplemented by the help of the young people who will grow up in such a family as theirs will be.

On the other hand, nothing is so easy as to undermine this sense of responsibility, and draw the very sap out of a man's life.

Social conditions are never, in this view, determining and, of course, the idea of trying was interpreted in a counter-factual manner: if circumstances prevailed to defeat a man's purpose it could mean only that his effort was insufficient.

The status of COS principles

So far the main arguments in the controversy have been described from the point of view of their basic content. Not only are they of substantive interest; they also centre on questions essential to any notion of social work – the place of moral judgment, the kind of morality assumed, notions of moral and civic responsibility. But value questions are not only or exclusively questions of morality, and the controversy sheds some light on problems of distinguishing between the elements usually left in an undifferentiated condition. For the arguments between the COS leadership and their critics also concerned questions about the status of the principles on which the COS claimed to be grounded: their source, immutability and their logical type.

The COS is often cited as a progenitor of modern social work, and it is not difficult to trace connections. It is, however, important to note that whereas its critics stressed the role of specialised and discrete professional treatments, one tendency in the COS was to ground the skill of the social worker in a heightened awareness of and a greater expertise in the ordinary business of moral and civic life. The Archbishop of Canterbury correctly identified this perspective as central when he said to the 1891 annual general meeting:

> You believe that what is the unhappy, suffering, miserable, neglected part of society has to be brought in within the rules and habits of civilisation and social life, has to be built up by exactly the same means, and in the same ways, and upon the same principles as those by which the present consolidated and self-supporting society has been brought together. (Reported *Charity Organisation Review*, June 1891)

Such a unified and consensual approach was, according to the critics, doomed to failure: the bond between helper and helped was non-existent or flawed. So for Townshend (1911), 'a capitalist class with a civilisation of its own cannot enter into the everyday life of wage-earner, who lives from hand to mouth, with habits, necessities and pleasures entirely different'. Whilst Hobson believed that though the well-to-do could because of temperament establish with the poor kindly personal relations, their superiority would be revealed and they were not capable of working along 'scientific' lines. He also considered that many such people shrank from close personal contact with concrete cases of suffering: they might give to charity, but the bond between donor and recipient was not established; 'the outward acts are entirely severed from the inward grace, and charity stagnates' (Hobson, 1909).

The principles governing charity would, in Hobson's view, be genuinely at work in a changed society. For such COS thinkers as C. S. Loch, however, the laws of social progress had already been discovered, and such laws yielded unchanging principles of action or, as he expressed it, 'prince thoughts, thoughts of highest or first rank, thoughts that command. These keep one steadfast when the world rocks.' Such principles were, according to Loch, unchanging, and he resisted the common criticism of the day that the COS was clinging to principles widely agreed to be out of date. For example, he rebutted Canon Barnett's well-intentioned criticism by charging him with being interested merely in fashion in welfare. 'He must be in harmony with the current philanthropic moment or perhaps just a few seconds ahead of it.' Loch would doubtless have been satisfied to read in C. R. Ashbee's satirical novel *The Building of Thelema* that the warden of the Settlement of St Saviour (a character modelled on Barnett) was called the Reverend Flux.

Yet the view that the COS should have changed with the times deserves more attention, since it opens up a general question concerning the continuous identity of social work and whether such an identity is to be found in a continuing though also modifying tradition of values. Woodard (1971) has argued from a historical viewpoint that the COS extolled the values of thrift and self-maintenance, and emphasised the folly of attempting to break the 'natural' connection between moral failings and their 'social' punishment at the most inappropriate historical time, when these qualities and concepts were no longer required. Towards the end of the nineteenth century economists extended to the subject of poverty the views of the classical political economists, such as Nassau Senior, of wealth as essentially amoral and guided by laws outside man's control. In this perspective the ideal type of the classical political economists, the man of diligence, thrift and temperance, was no longer relevant. However, the charge levied by the critics we are considering, that the leadership of the COS was out of joint with the times, was seen less in terms of economic change and more in terms of a change in the climate of political ideas, a shift in the perceived locus of social responsibility. So Barnett (1895) complained that the COS showed 'no sign of considering how the changed conditions of the time – the new consciousness of national possession – the new sense of inheritance of divine rights would affect the receipt, and does affect the refusal of such relief'. Similarly, Mrs Townshend (1911) observed,

> if only the leaders of the society had seen that the efficacy of charity for the redress of social grievances was at an end, and that the time had come when the community as a whole must shoulder its responsibilities the C.O.S. might have begun work of great national importance in preparing the way for modern social legislation.

These – and other – critics believed not only that the COS leadership had failed to read the signs of the changing political times, but also that the COS created trouble for themselves through what would now be termed certain category mistakes. They noted at least two. First, whilst the COS emphasised the factual basis of their experience and the facts against which the various proposals for social legislation should be tested, according to their critics, they ignored one special category, namely social facts. As Hobson argued, 'they confine themselves wholly to facts in their bearing on individual cases, ignoring those facts which consist in the relation of individual to individual. . . . All larger social and economic facts are consistently excluded from this view'. This was not, of course, what the COS intended. It explicitly acknowledged at least two problems concerned with the relation of the individual case to wider groupings: how to devise rules for work with cases considered exceptional and unsuitable for the broader rules and cruder identification of the Poor Law; how to consider each case on its merits whilst also considering 'in the individual case, what the more general effects of its action would be if carried out on a large scale in similar cases'

(Charity Organisation Paper, 1881). These problems are of significance beyond the period in question, and Hobson's observation
indicates that any conception of social work has to come to terms
with 'social facts' however this complex idea is understood.

The second category mistake concerned the way in which the
COS misinterpreted the status of their working rules, giving them a
significance out of all proportion. This mistake was formulated in
different ways by the critics. Barnett (1895) considered that the
COS Council had 'not been free of this tendency to set value on the
expression of the principle rather than on the principle itself'. Mrs
Townshend (1911) believed that the 'creed [i.e. full investigation,
adequate relief, no relief to the undeserving], which like all sets of
working rules, arose out of temporary conditions, many of them
badly needing alteration, has gradually acquired a kind of sacred
character, and a strange structure of social theory has been built on
it that is almost grotesque when compared with everyday experience'. Hobson argued that 'From the narrow empirical rules they
ascend to principles, or perhaps it would be more true to say, they
interpret their rules in the light of superimposed and externally
derived principles.' There are interesting differences between these
formulations, but broadly they suggest that the COS had mistaken
the logical form to be given to some of their central guiding notions,
and that they clung to this misperception against the evidence.

2 THE FUNCTIONALIST AND THE DIAGNOSTIC SCHOOLS OF SOCIAL CASEWORK

The controversy between these two schools of thought is probably
the least familiar of the three to be considered. It was largely
confined to America, receiving only slight and unsystematic attention in this country (though somewhat later the idea of agency
function was taken up and used by a few British writers),[1] despite
the fact that the Fulbright scholars in social work who came to
Britain regularly after the Second World War from America were
almost exclusively of a Diagnostic persuasion. The fierceness of the
controversy abated by the end of the 1950s, though work of a
specifically and acknowledged Functionalist orientation continued
to be produced in the following decade, when a functionalised view
was enlarged to characterise social work as a whole rather than

simply social casework. Smalley, for example, formerly Dean of the main Functionalist School at the University of Pennsylvania, published in 1967 *Theory for Social Work Practice*, which is based upon a Functionalist approach. By then, however, social work rejoiced in theoretical pluralism, and Smalley's contribution was offered 'in a spirit . . . not of defending, but of defining, a point of view'.

What might be gained from a study of this past, seemingly rather parochial episode? As with the other controversies it is possible to see how in a distinct historical period social workers conduct arguments about the nature of social work, referring either explicitly or implicitly to 'values'. This particular controversy, for example, revolves centrally around ideas of client freedom and the liberty of the citizen, and the role of choice and decision in the 'treatment' of those using social services. It also in its substantive content reveals a number of general problems in a discussion of value-talk in social work. First, quite simply but significantly, the usage of a common set of terms does not guarantee that the same use is being made of the terms. So, a professional committee appointed to seek common ground between the Functionalists and the Diagnostic School reported:

> Such jointly held concepts as (1) relating to the needs of the
> client, (2) applying psychological knowledge to gain an
> understanding of the client, and (3) utilizing the dynamics of the
> relationship to foster psychological growth, did not lend
> themselves to meaningful comparisons as separate entities since
> they were found to have quite different connotations when
> viewed within the context of the underlying premises of each
> group. (Kasius (ed.) 1950, p. 7)

Second, at least some of the Functionalists believed that the Diagnostic School implicitly held values that contradicted the democratic traditions of social work. This is of interest in itself, and also raises a general question concerning values that may be said to be implied in a theoretical position or to be held implicitly rather than explicitly.

The Functionalist School

The origin of the Functionalist School in the School of Social Work at the University of Pennsyslvania, and, significantly, in its network of social agencies, owes most to the work of two women, Virginia Robinson and Jessie Taft, and mainly through the latter, the psychological ideas of Otto Rank, a Freudian schismatic whose theory emphasised the will to growth and the enduring effects of the birth trauma. The two most important early documents are Virginia Robinson's *A Changing Psychology in Social Casework* (1930) and Taft's article 'The Relation of Function to Process in Social Casework' (1937). Robinson's book, though short, is currently neglected, but it constitutes one of the most crucial and, at the time of its publication, influential statements of a new position in social casework, which stressed both relationship and process. These ideas are now commonplace, even jejune, though they are not always well articulated or elaborated with imagination. Yet it was novel in the 1930s to argue that social casework had a unique contribution to make and that only in the field of the individual's reaction patterns and in the possibility of therapeutic change in these patterns 'through self-conscious relationships, can there be any possibility of a legitimate casework field'. To base the identity and the future of the only partially identified method of social work on a process of relationships and to endow that process with considerable authority was an innovation.

Such an innovation obviously advanced the interest of social casework as a profession in its own right and, as such, would appeal to any caseworker irrespective of orientation. What was distinctive about the Functionalist School was the claim that the skill of the social caseworker was not that of a psychiatric auxiliary, but a skill entirely *sui generis* based on a conception of a special process (of helping rather than of healing) and the active use of the principle of agency function which gave the process form and also linked both client and social caseworker to wider societal puposes, without making these dominant. Each of these ideas was developed in Taft's article to which reference has been made:

> There is one area and only one in which outer and inner, worker and client, agency and social need can come together effectively; only one area that offers to social workers the possibility of developments into a profession – and that is the area of helping process itself.

This process was one of helping and not one of psychotherapy or even of psycho-social treatment in any strong sense, and the main factor differentiating the helping process of social work from these other forms of intervention was the conscious recognition and use of what was termed 'agency function'. This notion obviously gave the school its name, and it was formulated in Taft's article in 1937. Taft, looking back some twenty years later, described 'agency function' in terms of a genuine discovery – and few of these have been described in social work. In a letter to another Functionalist, Ruth Gilpin, Taft said:

> The article on function has, perhaps, too much emotion in it, because actually the realization of function and its role in helping was a discovery for me, a genuine revelation. Also it fitted my bottom nature as relationship fitted Miss Robinson's. I think it was a little the way Rank felt when he realized 'will'. It illuminated everything.[2]

These are, of course, recollections in tranquillity of a determined pioneer, and it is now more widely recognised that the idea of agency function is as illuminative of questions as it is of answers. This is to amplify rather than dismiss its importance.

The idea of agency function as developed by the Functionalist School was complex, but it is worth describing in a little more detail since the main intention of the school was to re-establish social casework in some kind of context of social accountability, which, as we have seen, the COS attempted to formulate. Social caseworkers by definition were not free-lance or private practitioners, just as their clients were not 'abstracted' individuals simply choosing between commodities. The Functionalists believed that the social agency to which people came for different kinds of help was not a backcloth against which a therapeutic encounter was enacted. Taft (1944, p. 10) wrote of the agency as 'a background, which *holds* both worker and client in a larger reality' (italics added). The worker is identified not with the client but with the task or tasks for the accomplishment of which 'society' has sanctioned the agency and allocated to it certain resources. The client is envisaged not as a sick person asking for or requiring treatment for an illness, but as someone seeking a specific service (e.g. full or partial alternative care for a child). Functionalists believed that agencies were socially sanctioned to offer specific services (e.g. day minding for children), and also that the particular services should remain constant, as it were, for each particular client. Potential helpfulness was in the entity of the service. Services might change as distinct needs were generally recognised, but at any one time service or services entailed certain provisions and also a form of experience that was psychologically characteristic of giving and taking help in terms of that specific service.[3] This last characteristic is not easy to grasp, but what seems central is the idea that services are not commodities simply delivered to recipients more or less willing to accept them. The service might be of a tangible kind, but it is presented and offered in a way that invites the potential recipient to participate in a set of experiences intrinsically related to the service. For instance, a child may be emotionally rejected by his parents, who may take him to an agency that offers fostering or to a child guidance clinic: the 'problem' and the 'people' are the same in either situation, but according to the Functionalists each service entails a distinct set of experiences which take a form characteristic of the particular service and of its significance to client and community. A quotation from Taft (1944, p. 265) will show how the different elements in agency function cohere:

> it is never just the worker who is the source of the service, but agency itself, with its community roots and its varied resources. . . . When there is no separating and, at the same time, supporting medium, such as the social agency supplies, – no application process through which the applicant may test relation to agency and to the service he apparently seeks – there is, in my opinion, no place for the social worker. He himself may become the service, as the therapist does, but he no longer operates in his own unique profession.

The Diagnostic School

The Diagnostic School, centred on the Columbia School of Social Work, was also anxious to enhance the role and status of the social caseworker, but it tended towards the position in which the social worker was the service or at least was responsible for the major decisions in the offering and the delivery of service. For the Diagnostic School, service was a most carefully measured response to need, and the presence and the degree of need were a matter of and for professional judgment. The Diagnostics were more positive and less sceptical than their critics: need, in their view, could be known more or less exactly and could be directly worked on, whereas the Functionalists accepted 'the generally recognised categories [of social services] as they emerge out of the larger social problems and [left] to the individual the freedom as well as the responsibility of testing out his peculiar needs against the relatively stable function of a particular agency' (Taft, 1937).

The Diagnostic School adopted a flexible approach to agency services, which should ideally, in their view, be very finely tuned to individual need established in as much detail as possible. The centre of operations was, as the name of the school suggests, diagnosis of the problem. The diagnosis, in terms derived mainly from psychoanalytical theorising, extended to personality type, stage of psycho-social and psycho-sexual development, characteristic defence mechanisms, level of maturity and so on. The extent of diagnosis was significant, and so were the implied roles of expert diagnostician and of a client willing to be subjected to, persuaded or somehow manoeuvred into a process of study whereby his situation was categorised according to a taxonomy of which he remained largely unaware. Diagnosis also went hand-in-hand with the concept of treatment as a prescribed course of action and re-action or a distinctive repertoire of acts of intervention designed to cure or to alleviate. So, in 1938, Lowry, a teacher at the Columbia School of Social Work, outlined three types of treatment: manipulation, directed towards the enrichment or modification of the environment; environmental treatment, concerned with modifying the environment in order to affect individual relationships; and intensive or therapeutic treatment aimed directly at the modification of attitudes and relationships (quoted Gilpin, 1963, p. 20). Others distinguished between types of 'treatment' of a personal kind, so an 'insight'-giving approach was different from a supportive regime according to which comparatively intense and certainly long-term dependence on the social worker might be justified. Such an approach was criticised severely by the Functionalists, who themselves made use of the term 'diagnosis', but only just:

> We understand diagnosis, then, not as a categorizing of the
> client's make-up, with a resultant prescription for his needs,
> from the view point of an adjusted personality, but an attempt
> on the part of worker and client to discover whether client need

and agency service can be brought into a working connection that is mutually acceptable. The diagnosis is made when worker and client arrive at a plan for continuing and finally terminating the contract. (Taft, 1944, p. 8)

For the Functionalists diagnosis as described by the Diagnostic School was from a human point of view both an attempt at the impossible and an actual imposition.

Irreconcilability of the two schools

At the height of the controversy the two schools were judged to be irreconcilable. It is worth giving some attention to the reasons advanced in support of this view, not only because of the intrinsic interest of the particular debate but also because the question of the conciliation of opposing orientations is of more general interest in the study of social work values. Many individuals at the time of the earlier controversy between the COS leadership and 'the Socialists' believed that they could support and hence reconcile in some way both views. It is claimed that the arguments between the Functionalists and the Diagnostics resulted in some kind of fusion of ideas of each orientation, so that a writer like H. H. Perlman is seen as combining an emphasis on agency function with a psycho-social view of treatment and diagnosis. A first step in understanding such apparent marriages between what had been considered incompatible is to study the grounds on which instances of irreconcilability have been declared. The Functionalist–Diagnostic controversy provides one such case.

In 1950 a committee established by the Family Service Association of America (FSAA) to study basic social casework concepts reported on their comparison of Diagnostic and Functionalist ideas. They found that the 'two orientations cannot be effectively reconciled or combined' (Kasius (ed.), 1950, p. 13) in three crucial areas: personality structure, methods of work, and degree and kind of responsibility assumed. In relation to personality structure, the Functionalist School followed the theories of Otto Rank, which stressed the inborn will to individuation and individual autonomy. The 'will' organises inner and outer experiences to create the self or the ego, and the most pressing task of 'the will' is to achieve a sense of a separate self which is related to other selves, and to negotiate approaches towards people whilst maintaining the strong and separate sense of self. The Diagnostic School, on the other hand, followed a more orthodox Freudian approach in which 'will' was not of major significance, and the ego (rather than the self) is conceived as the product of the interaction of inner and outer forces. The committee went on to give some examples of the implications of these two sets of ideas about personality structure, and these are of interest in view of their useful observation that, depending on one's orientation, the same term could carry different meanings.

So, 'projection' was a term used by both schools. However, those of a Diagnostic persuasion used the term in the usual Freudian sense to refer to a particular defence mechanism whereby feelings of an unacceptable kind were disowned and 'put into' or 'put on' another person. Functionalists, on the other hand, used 'projection' differently in the context of a person pursuing a project: it described the release of inner impulses upon an outer object, and the appropriation of that object in self-interest. Similarly, 'resistance' was used differently by each school. The Diagnostics used the term to refer to an unconsciously imposed obstacle to self-understanding or insight which had as such to be overcome. Functionalists saw the matter differently. Resistance was the necessary effort of the will to maintain control in a situation in which the demand to change might get out of hand: new experiences in the helping process might help a client to relinquish such a use of his will, but resistance was not a direct target of therapeutic effort.

Differences between the schools in terms of methods of work have already been indicated. In the opinion of the committee of the FSAA, the Diagnostic School sought information about a client's total personality structure, whereas the Fuctionalists focused on the struggle in the client's will; for them what was crucial was the present expression of feeling valued primarily for its meaning to the client in the 'here and now' rather than as furnishing items of information for a full diagnostic portrait. The Diagnostics saw treatment as planned and goal-directed and not as 'as experience in form'. They took responsibility for a plan of treatment aimed at helping the client to approximate to a behavioural norm; they accepted the task of assessing individual capacity and of choosing between interventions directed at self-development and those of a more supportive nature. For them treatment was irresponsible

unless it was based on and directed by a diagnosis. The Functionalists interpreted their responsibilities in a different light. The central
core of casework was a personal relationship – and this begins to
sound similar to the view of their opponents – but the relationship
was of a particular kind, namely one in which the client could give
direction to his own processes of change. The client's choices and
goals in the helping process, and the outcome of that process, were
the responsibility of the client. The worker had the responsibility of
offering the service.

These differences – in psychological underpinning, methods of
work and degree of responsibility – it was agreed by the committee,
which contained representatives of each school, divided in irreconcilable ways Diagnostics from Functionalists. These differences
were later, as we have suggested, seen as less divisive or perhaps not
of great importance, though such ideas as 'agency function' were
received into more general currency in a considerably weaker form.
However, an even stronger case for irreconcilability was made in
the course of the controversy when attention was directed less to the
explicit positions adopted and more to what each school assumed.
The best example of this approach is to be found in an article by
Keith-Lucas (1953) apparently not accepted in the usual range of
social work journals. In it he argued that the assumptions of the
Diagnostic School pointed towards an essentially undemocratic
political theory. The article was largely ignored by other social work
journals, but it is of interest in the general consideration of social
work values because it provides an example of the explication of
what is implied and also because of the themes Keith-Lucas pursues
in analysing differences between the schools – different models of
human nature, distinct views on the knowledge social workers claim
and hence the degrees of control they seek to exercise, and differences in responsibility accepted.

Keith-Lucas argued that the Diagnostic School assumed that man
is by nature irrational and that he must, because of this, be helped to
choose; when he has chosen, after receiving the appropriate help
and perhaps insight, his choice would be what he would have chosen
were he rational. In exercising choice a man's right, according to
Diagnostic thinking, is dependent on the caseworker acting as some
kind of direct representative of society. This school, according to
Keith-Lucas, accepted responsibility for the client's whole personality and for devising treatment goals; it conceived of man as rational

only when he is adjusted to reality, and claimed scientific knowledge of human development and human action. On the other hand, argued Keith-Lucas, the Functionalists adopted a political theory much nearer to the democratic. They saw man as rational and capable of choice; the outcome of the helping process of social work was in any particular case unpredictable, and this was an inevitable characteristic in view of human nature. The Functionalist social worker accepted responsibility within carefully defined limits, in relation to the helping process and presenting agency function with regard to a particular problem. No claims were made, in a Functionalist perspective, to scientific knowledge of human nature, though the methods used were considered empirically valid.

Conclusions

As in the case of the first of the controversies considered, some of the terminology used by the Functionalists or the Diagnostics may appear primarily of historical interest. Some of the issues now may not even command concentrated attention, but many of the questions raised, if not pursued, are of a continuing interest. The Functionalists believed that they were reasserting important traditions in social work and that in contrast the Diagnostic School was hitching the rising star of therapeutic casework to the powerful medical constellation. They were conscious of the historical and the present roots of social work in the community, though they left largely undeveloped their preliminary ideas of the importance of *societally* sanctioned resources and auspices and of the crucial links between social work and society. Instead of pursuing the notion and the influence of traditions in social work (unhelpfully compressed in contemporary discussion into the simple and singular 'traditional social work'), they concentrated, rather like their opponents, on the relationship as *the* core of the helping process and on the development of self-understanding.

The value the Functionalists placed on self-knowledge derived from the high valuation given to a particular conception of the human personality. 'Each individual', wrote Smalley from a Functionalist perspective some time after the period of controversy, 'each bearer and sharer of the human condition, began with the first stirring of life on earth and, before that time, as part of the mystery of life's origin. He constitutes an expression of life force which has been unbroken since life began.' Their ideas of the personality, and their emphasis on the valuation of purpose and of the difference between one person and another, were sometimes expressed in a difficult prose style, and many writers of this school do seem to have placed high value on obscurity, recognising rather too eagerly the difficulties of 'forcing into the mould of logical and watertight definition that which defies every attempt to define' (Faatz, 1953, p. 5).[4] Nonetheless, they were clear that their conception of personality was not an ideal of any kind, as in the Diagnostic notion of the well-adjusted person: people in contact with social workers *are* part of the life force, pursuing purposes and struggling to establish individual differences.

The emphasis given to individual choice by the Functionalists may gain them some support from the contemporary reader, but this may be at the expense of disregarding the unrelenting nature of their pursuit of choice. For the Functionalist choice had almost an existential quality, were it not for the 'holding' and 'constraining' agency function. Certainly, choice was something one struggled towards, something one earned the hard way. The Diagnostic placed less value on choice and believed in differential treatment, in treating people in different situations differently. This was to them the basis and the height of a social worker's responsibility. They believed, no less firmly than the Functionalists, in establishing the profession of social work, but this entailed taking detailed responsibility for devising treatment and being concerned with the differential outcome of different treatments. They agreed with their opponents about the source of working rules (mainly psychological theory), but they differed from them in the way in which the client was seen as the expert in relation to his or her situation and as the source of an authorised/authentic decision to accept or to reject the service. Each school valued the independent and the dependent character differently: the Functionalists were stern upholders of the self that must be self-determining if it is to be a self; the Diagnostics were less rigorous, perhaps more paternalistic. The former respected the core of self-determination in a person, even when in ambivalence the person concerned might not be very enthusiastic about being self-determined. The latter had perhaps more respect for the particular condition in which humans may find themselves. Both schools, however, were concerned to work with individuals.

'In this respect', wrote Faatz, a Functionalist writer who came to British attention largely through quotations from her work used to good, if rather easy, critical advantage by Wootton (1959), 'namely, that casework is devoted to the one, to the importance of the single, separate life expression, there can be no difference of opinion.' (There can, of course, be such difference, and the next controversy to be discussed reveals this.)

The controversy between the Functionalists and the Diagnostics indicates, then, questions of a continuing importance in social work. It also raises a general problem for any study of 'values', namely, how should account be taken of values, valuation, or value judgments that can be described as implicit? It is, of course, relatively easy to state implicit presence; and more difficult to show it, to the satisfaction of observers, if not of participants. Yet, because it is difficult to become aware of values, valuations and sometimes value judgments, we cannot rule out the notion of 'the implicit'. The onus, it seems to me, is on the observer or commentator. He or she has to show some kind of entailment, not necessarily of a strict logical nature, between what A says and/or does and what A has not said or done but B says is implied. This entailment can be of several kinds: B may try to show that a reordering of A's tenets offers a more complete or a sounder basis for A's position; B may seek to demonstrate that A's position is untenable or incomprehensible except in terms of what is implied. Yet any such questions of entailment require dialogue between A and B, and the Diagnostic School maintained almost total silence in the face of the analysis of their position as implicitly undemocratic.

3 RADICAL SOCIAL WORK

Introduction

Something of the flavour of this current, only partly mounted, controversy can be sensed from a quotation from a recent, somewhat hasty attempt at the demolition of social work:

> One of the most heartening aspects of the extreme radical wing of social work (at least to their opponents) is their almost total inability to deliver their revolutionary message in words

comprehensible to anyone save second-rate graduates in second-rate sociology – usually a matter of preaching to the converted. Less heartening is the ability of authors who appear to hover on the edge of literacy to command hard covers. (Brewer and Lait, 1980, pp. 106–7)

Abuse is not confined, of course – 'radicals' have criticised opposing views in strong terms as simplistic, myopic, idealistic and so on – but the quotation helps us to gauge something of the currency of the idea of radical social work. It also identifies the villain of the piece – though it is doubtful if these particular critics or others can recognise sociology, let alone grade it – and assumes perhaps that 'radical social work' is both a recent and a unitary phenomenon. By way of introduction I would like to comment on these possible characteristics by attending to the description 'radical' as applied to social work. A social work that was radical would propose not only changed methods of intervention but also different values.

'Radical' is sometimes operationally defined in terms of a contrast. So a 'radical', whatever else he or she may be, is not a reformer: he or she does not espouse reform as a cause, but seeks something beyond or qualitatively different from reform. The radical wishes to make a completely fresh start, to make anew, whereas the reformer wants to improve existing patterns or at least some of them. This way of understanding a radical person or a radical approach does not of itself say anything about the general political direction towards which the root changes point. Presumably, all radicals would see the direction in which they propose to travel as a forward one, but as Chekhov once observed, if you say 'Forward' to a revolutionary and an orthodox monk, they will travel in precisely opposite directions. A radicalism of the political right is no less coherent than a radicalism of the political left, though in ordinary conversation it is often assumed that 'radical' must refer to someone on the far left of the political spectrum. This is not to say that nothing distinguishes the two potential directions of radicalism: the radical of the Right is, for example, perhaps more likely to recognise that revolutions are comprehensible as a result of the reassertion of a hidden, submerged tradition. However, at this stage in the argument, the most important point to be made in relation to social work concerns a tension or temptation common to both radical positions. A radical characteristically hovers on the borderline that separates radical change in direction or conception from the total remodelling of the original institutional form or set of arrangements so that they are changed out of all possible recognition. Applying this perspective to social work leads to the question, are radicals concerned to change the form of social work, so that it is recognisable as radical social work or as a social work that is radical compared to the social work that is now recognisable as social democratic? Or does a radical approach leave no room for social work in any form recognisable as social work by insisting that it should change into something completely different?

The present debate about the very idea of a radical social work should attend not only to the coherence of the notion but also to the historical development of social work. It is significant, and puts the present controversy into some perspective, that social work and social workers have, at different periods, described themselves or have been described by others in radical terms since the late nineteenth century. It probably appears perverse to think of the COS in these terms, but there is this to be said in favour of C. S. Loch's description of the Society as essentially progressive: the attempt to use the idea of the common life of citizenship as a basis for social welfare marked a decisive break with some earlier Christian formulations. Seen as the attempt to create an alternative to the rough bargaining and the approximations of reciprocity and the strict complementarity of rights and duties, it could indeed be viewed as radical. Similarly, the Functionalists saw themselves in a radical light in so far as they broke with Freudian tradition in the interests of freeing their clients; and early child guidance clinic social workers would have used the ideas of Freud to liberate their clients from the oppression of the super-ego. Other social workers in that era would also have seen themselves, at least in professional terms, as radicals. Thus, Reynolds (1951), from the base of social work practice in connection with a trade union in America, came to ask radical questions concerning the received practical wisdom of the profession. For example, it was commonly assumed that seeking and obtaining help was by its very nature painful. Reynolds asked the simple question 'Must it hurt to be helped?' and replied in terms not of psychological process or personality features but of the characteristics of organisations and the types of social relations they encouraged: helping did not inflict inevitable pain if worker and client were in fraternal relations in a brotherly organisation.

In Britain a well-established line of criticism urging social work to make a radical change in direction stretches from Baroness Passfield to Baroness Wootton. The opinion of the former is quoted in *A Socialist View of Social Work*, published some twenty years ago: 'Are social workers willing accessories to what Beatrice Webb referred to as "pulling people out of the swamp when they should be draining it?" The answer to this question involved an important differentiation:

> It is essential to distinguish between what is a professional task – namely, to give the best possible service within the framework of the agency or service – and what is a political task – namely, to bring about improvements in the scope and function of the service itself. Socialists would approve of an increase in social workers to help individuals to develop their potential in a valid and creative way and to take part in research on social problems; but they should oppose the use of social workers to persuade people to tolerate what is clearly intolerable.

Just as in the past, as we have now seen, social workers have considered themselves or have been considered as 'radicals' on different grounds and in distinct historical contexts, so the term is currently applied to a number of groupings of distinguishable orientations. Take, for example, a recent collection of essays, *Radical Social Work and Practice*, ed. Brake and Bailey. This brings together *as* radical such different approaches as the kind of Marxism evident in the editorial introduction; advocacy of a perspective on feminism which, it is claimed, is not fully explicable in terms of class oppression; and the views of a contributor, 'much persuaded by the insights of Marxist analysis, but nevertheless committed to democratic solutions', who believes in a piecemeal revolution and in the idea that a radical social work practice grows out of the radical personality. The notion of a radical personality is arresting, but on closer examination appears more familiar.

> In and out of the job the radical personality will not be pushed around by officials; will not remain silent when it/he is aggrieved; will be aware and unafraid of change; will be thoroughly conversant with the political nature of most taken-for-granted tactics and behaviour.

Now, the point is not to ask what kind of personality could or should remain unafraid of change he or she had good reason to regard as fearful (not all change is good; not every need or strength should be encouraged), but to note the very broad range of ideas that are currently defined as radical.

In the face of the considerable diversity of views that are described as radical, it is sensible to focus on one particular orientation. This is not because any one tradition alone has a right to the description but because some concentration enables questions relevant to the study of social work values to be more clearly discussed. The view I have decided to discuss in this last section on controversy is that of the Marxists who propose a form of social work requiring to be informed not by a view of the status of clients (as fellow citizens) nor by a view of the nature of the process in which clients and social workers are engaged (the helping process), but by an entirely new notion of personality and of society and of the accompanying ideas of morality and politics. Such drastic changes are of interest in themselves, but discussion of a Marxist approach to social work also directs attention to a number of general questions significant in the study of social work values. In particular, exploration of a Marxist approach cannot avoid issues of context. Not only do Marxists emphasise the historical context in which ideas about social work values might arise, but the very project of a Marxist social work involves the application of ideas taken from a Marxist context which is both complex and contested – even within Marx and Marxism. Moreover, a Marxist approach to social work suggests as important topics the idea and the reality of compromise and the difficulties people of different political 'ideologies' have in even understanding each other. It helps us to ask 'Why be moral?' and raises important questions about what constitutes morality. It tests crucially the individualism prominent in the other controversies considered in this chapter. First, however, we should consider as a question the very possibility of a social work that is Marxist.

Marxist social work – is it possible?

It is only quite recently that such a possibility has been argued persuasively and in some detail, other than for demolition purposes. This is not surprising. The writings of Marx are massive in volume and of intricate complexity. As Walton and Gamble (1972) have argued:

> It is not simply a question of the quantity and complexity of Marx's work, but that much of it is written in different styles, with a varied audience or, as in the case of the Grundrisse, no audience in mind. It is not just that the *Economic and Philosophical Manuscripts* are different from the Grundrisse, which in turn is different from *Capital*, but also that, taken individually, none are really complete. (p. 25)

They argue that because of these characteristics one cannot understand Marx without understanding the Marxists. No Marxist of international standing has sought to develop the ideas on social welfare to be found in rudimentary form in Marx's original writings. Mishra's (1981) sympathetic (but non-Marxist) account of a possible Marxian perspective on social policy shows how much construction has to be undertaken before anything like general shape is clear. If this is the case in relation to social welfare generally, despite Marx's detailed knowledge of and interest in such a specific area as factory legislation, how much more work is required to establish even an outline of Marxist social work?

Yet the difficulty in establishing a Marxist social work derives not simply from the extensive nature of the work of Marx nor from what Mishra calls the arbitrary decision of 'whom one includes under the rubric of "Marxist" ' (1981, p. 88). It derives also from the fact that many of the notions crucial to the form and to the justification of social work are deeply controversial within Marxism – ideas such as 'freedom', 'morality', 'human' and so on. It is, moreover, contestable within Marxism whether or not there can be such a thing as post-revolutionary social work. Bolger *et al* (1981) state that 'Socialist welfare work is something that will have to be struggled for and defended even when the mode of production is characterised by socialist forms', but it is unclear why in terms of a Marxist analysis this should be so. Finally, some argue that 'the objects of Marxist theory are specified by its own concepts: the mode of production, the class struggle, the state, ideology, etc.' and attempts to apply it to such pre-given fields of sociology as crime, education, the family (and presumably such manifestations as social work) are 'a more or less "revisionist" activity in respect of Marxism; it must modify and distort Marxist concepts to suit its own pre-Marxist purpose' (Hirst, 1975).

So, those who, to use a favoured word in this context, *struggle* to establish a Marxist social work face a number of problems internal to their general theoretical perspective. Not all Marx's central concepts are used and the choice between them has to be justified on some grounds or other. Corrigan and Leonard (1978), for example, decided 'not to put stress upon the concept of alienation' (p. 64) but do not argue a justification for their decision beyond mentioning the vulgarisation of the concept. In this and several other works we are offered no overall picture of the complexity of Marx's theory nor of the considerable controversy amongst Marxists concerning the meaning and the significance of major aspects and components of Marx's bold theoretical work. Miliband (1977) in a widely used text suggests that in general such a gap in presentation and understanding should not be considered at all troublesome. 'There are many worse slogans', he states, 'than "everyone his own Marx". For in the end there is no "authoritative" interpretation – only personal judgment and evaluation' (p. 5). Such ecumenism without a church has its attractions, but there must surely be *some* boundary separating Marx from not-Marx, and some answer to the question insistent within Marxism itself concerning the nature of the project on which Marx was engaged. The major concepts used in building Marxist social work – base and superstructure, ideology versus the dull compulsion of economic relations, and so on – are *controversial* amongst Marxists, and the controversies must affect how these ideas are to be treated in any context, including that of social work.

Marxists who write about social work are aware of some at least of the problems they face in achieving their aim of articulating a politically progressive social work in a capitalist society. 'The Marxist social worker who wants to practise a Marxist social work cannot *simply* do so precisely because of a bourgeois hegemony in theory and practice' (Corrigan and Leonard, 1978, p. 153; italics added). The dominance of one social class is achieved, so followers of Gramsci argue, not so much by the deliberate use of crude economic forces as through the powerful influence of a set of interconnected and, literally, ruling ideas and sentiments. If the dominance of particular ideas and institutions by a certain social class is a fact of any pre-revolutionary social life, then the rise of radical social work (along with many other potential threats to the order established through hegemony or the force of economic relations) appears problematic. The question is, how to account for the start, the growth and the possibilities of radical social work, except as an outlet sanctioned by the ruling class for the safe discharge of revolutionary fervour. Radical social workers adopt different solutions to the problem, though some (e.g. Brake and Bailey (eds), 1980) do not raise the issue. Corrigan and Leonard (1978) maintain that the state has a measure of autonomy in relation to the forces of social class and that contradictions within the state exist and should be exploited; attempts to use state workers (social workers) to force change that is progressive in the state apparatus should only be undertaken when the workers are part of a much wider coalition of class forces actually campaigning for change. However, the idea of relative autonomy does require squaring with 'contradiction'. Moreover, Thompson (1978), whilst welcoming relative autonomy as a 'helpful talisman against reductionism – against collapsing art or law or religion objectively back into class or "economics" ', argues that 'without substantial addition, and substantive analysis, it remains as nothing more than a warning-notice. Certainly, the hour of the last analysis never comes, if, by that hour, one supposes the total collapse of all human activities back into the elementary terms of a mode of production' (p. 289).

For Statham (1978), however, the problem of accounting for the rise and the flourishing of Marxist social work presents almost insuperable problems, and her solution to what is accurately described as the dilemma of the radical social worker raises further difficulties about compromise in social work and the compromised social worker. On the one hand, argues Southam, the results of social analysis undertaken in movements outside social work should be used by social workers. Too much, however, should not be expected of this – the practice of left-wing radicals in social work is strictly circumscribed. Despite these limitations, the attempt to apply the social analysis is worthwhile. On the other hand, the form of social work as a social formation is limited: 'institutionalized social work *cannot* have a revolutionary *function*, and, irrespective of their origin, ideas taken into it *have* to become liberalized – diverted of their revolutionary impetus' (italics added). (As Dr Johnson might have said, 'I have heard of revolutions, of course; even of revolutionary aspects, but revolutionary *functions* never!') How, then, can the fruits of revolutionary analysis survive, let alone flourish, once they have been incorporated into, or simply brought within the boundaries of, social work? Southam provides no answer to the question, but seems to define radical social workers as compromisers. Radicals who decide to remain in what she describes as traditional social work 'know that compromise, not purity is the rule'. Compromise does indeed seem to figure as an important element in social work, perhaps concerned with the ways in which rules are applied or purposes pursued, and it is to be distinguished from 'being compromised', but neither concept is developed in the writings of Marxist social work. Statham does develop the concept of compromise somewhat in a discussion of the inescapable demand that one should serve either a bourgeois or a socialist ideology. In her view the ideology of social work cannot be other than bourgeois in a society that remains pre-revolutionary. 'Although individuals within the profession may reject it they can remain within social work or, for that matter, in any other social institution through conscience compromise' (p. 36). The intrusion of this qualification raises questions about the meaning of 'compromise' but more importantly marks the arrival of moral considerations which, as we shall see, present particular problems for those who adopt a Marxist approach.

So, the feasibility of a 'genuinely' Marxist social work is not without problems, and it is not easy to discern its distinctive features: the characteristic words in this respect used by Marxist writers are 'beginnings' and 'struggle'. It is possible, however, to outline some of the main elements in an emerging Marxist social work by considering a number of related rules or maxims: work as much, if not more, outside as inside social work; avoid and undermine the cult of individualism; be wary of 'ideas'; do not be afraid of the notion and reality of contradiction.

Working and making allies outside social work

It would be a caricature to suggest that on occasion the message of Marxist social work could be reduced to one simple piece of advice: only connect – with trade unions. Yet trade unions occupy a special place in Marxist social work because they are simply taken to be working-class institutions and also potentially indispensable instruments of the revolution. Corrigan and Leonard acknowledge the lack-lustre quality of the proposition and also refer to the limitations that Lenin saw in trade union consciousness, but nonetheless they see alliance with trade unions as crucial. Other Marxists agree. 'The social worker not only needs to build up trade union *consciousness* within his/her own section, but also needs to develop links with other welfare state unions' (Brake and Bailey (eds), 1980, p. 19; italics added). The reasons offered for the formation and development of these links are interestingly varied. They afford protection for social workers: the links with trade unions 'can be used to improve the position of basic grade workers in the corporate management of local authority services' (*ibid.*, p. 20). Within a Marxist perspective altruism, unlimited or otherwise, is not required. Galper (1980) argues that radical social work does not ask the practitioner to be self-sacrificing to the point of self-destruction and notes, almost like a psycho-social caseworker of a different tradition, that practice which is adventuristic may primarily satisfy a psychological need. Links with trade unions also provide the trade union movement with detailed knowledge of the sufferings of those who are victims of an exploitive social system. Finally, they help to forge a coalition that may bring about change or may come to represent the interests of a working class conscious of itself: the links connect social workers with a movement that may come to represent the class that must, sooner or later, dominate.

Marxist social work is also concerned with the creation of other kinds of alliance. Social workers should become involved in radical issues and in community politics, not necessarily as a way of participating in a more extensive radical movement, but because such involvement is relevant to social work practice and offers the radical social worker much-needed support. An approach towards radical groups outside social work offers the social worker 'alternative views of reality, and emotional and ideological support. An obvious example is in the area of sexual politics, either in feminism or gay liberation. There are other groups involved in class politics, fighting racism, or sexual politics. Feminism is important because of its useful insights into the political importance of women in servicing the economy.' (Brake and Bailey (eds), 1980, p. 20). It does need to be shown, of course, precisely what these beneficial results are and in what their benefit consists. One may wonder also, with Martin Davies (1981), how long such wide-ranging political work will be tolerated by employing bodies under the description of social work. This question is not answered merely in terms of prudence and a glance at the conditions of service, since what is at issue is an intrinsic rather than a personal or an extrinsic aim of the social worker (to use a categorisation of Downie and Telfer (1980) to which reference has already been made).

Avoiding the cult of individualism

Establishing effective connections with unions and with other political movements is justified on a number of grounds: the potential pay-off in revolutionary terms; as a requirement of an essential part of the practice that is social work; as action that is collective, i.e. social group action. It is this last justification that connects the first maxim with the avoidance of the cult of individualism. The second maxim is complex, partly because of the long and varied history of individualism, but also partly because of the qualifications introduced through current analyses from a Marxist perspective.

For Marxist social workers a prime disvalue is to be found in the notion of individualism which is based on an essentially flawed understanding of the individual as somehow abstracted from any historical or social context, as an inescapable isolate, morally selfish, and simply not a social or a political animal. Individualism, which to some is a triumph, the end result of the long march of Everyman, is for the Marxist the extreme expression of alienation and privatisation; it is the dominance of the private arena over the obligations and metaphysics of solidarity. For Marxists 'the alienated individual' somehow takes over and assimilates rather than diversifies the species. Not all Marxists would agree with Althusser, who argues that individuals should be seen only as bearers of certain functions and not as subjects at all, but most Marxists are stronger on how 'individuals' are seen and understood and much weaker on individuals as bearing not functions but rights. In this situation no idea of individual rights is available to rescue men from what Thompson (1978) sees as the conservative tendencies implied in the idea of man as bearing certain functions, since this 'tends to see men and women as fixed in "stations", on ladders of "rank", subject to "laws" (of Smith or of Malthus), allocated "roles", or as *moments* of conformity or deviance within an ulterior consensus' (p. 339; italics added).

Marxist social workers do not face the full force of individual rights or of individuals described as bearing certain claims. They seem rather to assert two propositions: individuals should be interpreted in terms of something more 'basic', and any exclusively individualistic understanding is limited. So, Corrigan and Leonard (1978) state:

> We must begin to understand individual experience and the features of individual personality as a reflection of the social relations of production and of the contradictions within those relations. This means understanding them not only in relation to the family as a reflection, at least in part of the dominant economic structure, but also in the other wider structures with which individuals interact. In this way, the analysis that social workers undertake of individual and social situations is not then simply a dichotomy between understanding the individual and understanding the social structure. (p. 122)

There are, of course, other ways of overcoming this dichotomy than by seeing individual experience as a reflection or part reflection of something else: 'reflection' is a favoured term in Corrigan and Leonard, but it is left largely unanalysed. Similarly, their perception of 'exclusively individual understanding' as 'at best an alienated and limited form of consciousness' ignores the fact that in Marx such a form of consciousness is not so much limited as flawed, and leaves to be explored the proposition that social relations create the individual but also are created by *him*: Althusser would give the individual no such creative status.

Practically speaking, however, Marxist social workers are not opposed to all forms of social work with individuals. Galper (1980) argues that 'If counselling is required, it must be given'. However, it should be given only upon certain conditions, to be met and decided upon presumably by the social worker: 'if the counselling fails to link a specific and immediate problem with the social dynamics of which it is but one manifestation and if it fails to link the temporary and partial solutions with the larger social transformation that is required for realistic solutions, then it is extremely limited, at best, and deceptive and repressive, at the worst' (pp. 12–13). In terms of Marxist theory it is perhaps surprising that individual work has even 'extremely limited' point. Brake and Bailey (1980, p. 23) take a different approach: within a Marxist perspective the individually based work is quite simply transformed: 'traditional techniques such as casework, group work and family work, are given a new meaning and a new dimension when affiliated to a radical socialist perspective'. It is not easy to see the sort of affiliation they envisage, nor how the reworking of the individualistic approach which Corrigan and Leonard outline can be seen as a new *dimension*. The novelty proposed by Brake and Bailey is not easily grasped except as placing the individual problem in the framework of a new definition.

Beware 'ideas'

Marxists use 'idealist' as a term of negative criticism. 'Idealist' in this context refers not primarily to the person who can be described as 'an idealist', but rather to the possible dominance of ideas over those interests that spring directly from the material stuff of life, and for the Marxist such stuff is only to be seen in terms of the relations of production which derive from the material productive forces. Within social work the Marxist emphasis on the material of life poses a radical challenge in view of the historical origins of modern social work, which were heavily influenced, as we have seen, by the explicitly Idealist School of the late nineteenth century. Against this tradition modern Marxist social workers assert a contrary epistemology. Bernard Bosanquet emphasised the necessary contribution of 'right ideas' to material welfare, though contemporary Marxists may fail to appreciate that for Bosanquet knowledge hardly existed until the form it possessed 'in the book' was actually destroyed. Nonetheless, contemporary Marxists writing on social work stress experience rather than ideas.

In the current debate Marxists tend to assert an exclusive epistemology: there is only one way in which real or authentic knowledge can be gained. It cannot be gained from the position of 'outside': theory must derive from experience. This, in itself, may not be a remarkable proposition, depending on how we understand 'experience' and 'derived from', but the Marxist believes that, so far as social work is concerned, theory derives from particular kinds of experience:

If we are not black [or, presumably, male, born in a particular historical era, and so on], although we may participate in action,

> we cannot contribute to the *analysis* of black oppression,
> because, however enlightened our views are thought to be ['by
> whom?' is a useful question], the white are among the
> oppressors. (Statham, 1978, p. x)

It is not easy to see why such *a priori* positions are necessary: why
not see what any particular group's contribution to analysis
amounts to? Yet there is something crucial to the Marxist position
in the insistence that only certain kinds of experience legitimate
both understanding and intervention. For some Marxists participation in action to change reality is at least a necessary condition of
knowledge. Admittedly, this is, in a Marxist view, more often stated
than demonstrated (one is reminded of the frequency with which
followers of the psychoanalyst Melanie Klein talked of her dis-
coveries rather than her statements). Thus Corrigan and Leonard
(1978) rely on a simple unelaborated quotation from Mao Tse-
Tung:

> If you want to know a certain thing or class of things directly,
> you must personally participate in the practical struggle to
> change that thing or class of things, for only thus can you come
> into contact with them as phenomena. (p. x)

This quotation, however, poses problems. How can one directly
know *a class* of things? What are the grounds for saying that personal participation in the struggle to change reality *alone* guarantees
knowledge? How can you know that things should be changed if you
have no prior knowledge of them? Are the connections between
participation in the struggle psychological or logical? Why must it
be insisted that there is only one, sovereign way along which
phenomena can be met? Marxist imperialist sovereignty over ideas
cannot be won simply by assertion, particularly of a romantic kind.

The notion of contradiction

The idea of contradiction figures largely in accounts of Marxist
social work, and indeed in Marx. It seems to take a strong and a
weak form. The weak form we have already encountered in the
description of social work values (in Siporin; see p. 18, above) as
'both-and' values. In this form, two assertions are made or signalled,
and to some extent they qualify each other or even nullify each

other. Galper's work is a very good example of a balancing act (on the one hand . . . on the other hand . . .) which may be exciting for the spectator but is of limited instrumental use for the practitioner, unless he or she is an apprentice tight-rope walker. An illustration of the stronger version of contradiction is to be found in Bolger *et al* (1981), though they begin with the idea of contradiction in logic:

> in common parlance for a person to admit that their argument is built round a contradiction is to admit that they have a major problem in their argument, that they are not really consistent. For us, and for most Marxists, the concept of contradiction within social structures is essential. A contradiction within a structure must not be confused with a difference between one structure and another. A contradiction means that there are elements of that structure that can only be *fully* realised, can only be put into effect, by destroying other elements of that situation. This means that the structure is in *constant tension*, since simultaneously one part of the structure can only be successfully realised at the expense of another. (p. 3)

On the whole, the idea of contradiction is not applied by Marxists directly to social work: it is used to understand the society in which social workers play their part. However, the quotation from Bolger does show some of the difficulties of attaining a grasp on the idea: the relationship with logical contradiction is unclear; it seems easier to show what the signs of contradiction are than what the concept means; strong ideas of 'destruction' are placed alongside weaker notions of 'at the expense of'.

Conclusions

'Values' are treated seriously by some Marxist writers at least, but they are treated in an undifferentiated manner, even though implicit distinctions are made between objectives, ultimate goals and ideals, and those valuations that are instrumental in the preservation of a particular social order. There is a tension within Marxist writing on social work between reinterpreting the 'traditional' values and hence taking them seriously and dismissing the formulations as social myths whose main objective is the furtherance of 'real' economic valuations. However, the main challenge of the

Marxist consideration of values in social work lies in the refusal to settle for an abstract and an abstracted treatment, though in arguing for a reduction in the level of abstraction and for the essential contribution of the historical and social context, Marxist social work writers form common cause with critics of other orientations. A Marxist approach to 'values' also faces particular problems. These require solution, but also help us to see more clearly general problems that face any treatment of social work values and values of social work.

Two examples may help to illustrate this last point, and each refers to what is problematic within Marxism. Within Marxist social work writing there is a marked tendency to use as a central criterion the idea of 'the truly human'. Thus Corrigan and Leonard (1978) refer to 'creating the conditions which will enable a truly human practice to take place' (p. 141), or to 'insisting on a truly human response to suffering which confronts an inhuman society' (p. 157). Simpkin (1979, p. 1) believes that a radical approach will 'ensure the possibility of real personal encounters', whilst Brake and Bailey (1980, p. 23) use 'cruel' as one of the criteria for deciding against the use of vulnerable groups in society. However, humanistic notions are deeply controversial within Marxism – Althusser (1976), for instance, writes 'one can and must speak openly of *Marx's theoretical anti-humanism*. ... It is impossible to *know* anything about men except on the absolute precondition that the philosophical (theoretical) myth of man is reduced to ashes' (pp. 229–30). Moreover, Marxist social workers *rely* on the understanding of 'truly human', the main part of which must have 'liberal' foundations. Certainly, in the absence of a specifically Marxist interpretation of 'truly human', no other understanding is readily available.

The second example comes from the characteristic way in which Marxist social work writings treat the notion of human freedom as opposed to ideas of social, historical or material determinism. Social work to be social work is forced to attend to this issue: ideas of self-determination, client choice and so on simply fail and fall if the answer to the question 'Could he/she have done otherwise?' is negative in every conceivable instance. Again, the question is problematic within Marx's own writings, as well as within and without Marxism. Maguire (1978), like other commentators, contrasts what Marx wrote about particular historical events and the more general deterministic position he argued: 'Indeed, so far is he from a "mechanistic" or "reductive" approach when he actually deals with concrete problems, that the difficulty is to reconcile what he says about them with the kind of general claim which he wants to maintain' (p. 241). O'Rourke (1974) suggests that on the question of free will it is difficult to know where Marx stands: 'none of Marx's statements concerning the will carry sufficient precision or philosophical impact to constitute a properly philosophical position' (p. 45). Marxist writers only continue the ambiguous treatment by talking of that which is determined 'in the last resort'.

Finally, a Marxist approach to social work does seem to leave moral judgments and moral ideals in an uncertain state. Clearly, Marxist social work writers are moved by human suffering, and they condemn exploitation. They deny that they support the deterioration of present circumstances in order to facilitate the revolution, but it is difficult to see how they can avoid facing the fact that, in their perspective, what ought to be done is that which most advances the revolution. So, Corrigan (1975) argues against conventional moral judgments: 'selecting methodology of political work by means of morality will not lead to a correct solution. It may well be wrong to intervene in the class struggle from outside (assuming that community workers are déclassé) but the ways in which we judge it wrong or right are based upon the moral judgments of the world around us, the bourgeoisie.' In his view there is in opposition to bourgeois morality a communist morality which 'stems from the overall necessity for increasing the likelihood of change; a change that *can* only be carried out by the mass of the people'. Galper (1980, p. 67) argues that 'Violence against people is justified at the point at which there will be greater physical injury to revolutionary forces if violence is not employed.' The 'musts' that figure significantly in Corrigan and Leonard are never presented as moral: to behave insensitively is harmful not to persons but to one's own future interest in the revolution. This kind of approach to morality may well flow from the problematic treatment of morality in Marxism – where it is argued that Marx *is* morality or that only false (bourgeois) morality is possible in our pre-revolutionary society. However, it presents a particular problem in a social work that has always shown, even in a muddled way, deep moral seriousness and, as we have seen when considering conscience, offers little help to the social worker who asks in a particular situation, 'What ought I to do? At worst Marxist analysis suggests a version of ethical expediency; at best the moral sovereignty of one supreme human goal. The first offers nothing that could count as guidance. The blinding illumination of the second provides no steady light by which a course might be steered.

6

Values, valuations and value judgments I

One review of the literature . . . found some 400 works which referred explicitly to values and which encompassed no less than 180 different definitions of the term 'values'.

S. Harding (1980)

Values are, therefore, neither things nor experiences, nor essences; they are values.

R. Frondizi (1971), p. 6

The word *value* has an enormous variety of meanings which range all the way from the price of a commodity to the significance or the goals of human action.

Margenau and Oseanyan (1970)

Values reflect needs and interests, but are neither of these. Neither are values simply goals, though they may be, but criteria against which goals are chosen.

C. Patterson (1959)

Introduction

The argument so far has advanced through four stages. First, whatever one's understanding of social work, 'values' are given a central place in social work activity both in the exposition and in the justification of social work. Second, values, despite their agreed importance, have not been given the sustained and critical treatment warranted. This, it has been argued, is not a satisfactory situation: 'values' rendered into no distinguishable elements at all are expected to perform too many generalised tasks. Third, it is suggested that conceptual analysis, whether applied to the situation of the social worker making a moral decision or to the customary lists and listings of social work values, constitutes an important advance in securing an improvement on the present treatment of social work values. However, such analysis is a necessary not a sufficient condition for the success of the present enquiry, so the fourth stage of the argument concerned the historical contexts in which important differences between social workers have been recorded. Concepts cannot be considered to have been fully treated outside a historical context. The controversies, though briefly discussed, showed that, whilst the contenders did not always refer explicitly to 'values', they were concerned with different notions of what it is to be truly human, of human freedom and liberation and of the responsibilities and constituents of human sociability.

So far the argument has been conducted within the confines of social work, its concepts and history. Such an approach, as we have seen, produces its own problems, and these cannot be solved or even satisfactorily grasped on, as it were, a domestic basis. The fifth and final stage of the argument of this enquiry turns to an exploration of the treatment of value and values outside social work. As has already been stated, it is a justifiable criticism that social work values are usually discussed in a narrowly domestic fashion, and this and the following chapter aim to provide at least the beginning of a comparative exploration which will both sharpen awareness of shortcomings in value-talk in social work and indicate some remedies. It is, of course, easier to mount a response to the challenge of narrowness than to sustain it. To be 'outside' social work is not to be anywhere in particular; to occupy some vast territory where the problem is not so much the ease with which one can lose one's way as the difficulty of finding anything resembling a way in the first place. Those following distinct disciplines or speaking in no disciplinary sense at all, people in every walk of life and for many different purposes, all use the terms 'value' and 'values'. These terms are used with frequency and sometimes with a certain solemnity, particularly in academic discussions. As Charles Morris has observed: 'The term "value" is one of the Great Words, and, like other such words ("science", "religion", "art", "morality", "philosophy") its meaning is multiple and complex' (1956, p. 9).

Within the separate disciplines 'value' can be given a special status. So, Robinson (1964), who argues that it is only a word, believes that it expresses 'one of the great metaphysical ideas in economics' (p. 29).

Some sense of direction through the complexity surrounding 'value' and 'values' outside social work can be gained through recalling the rather instrumental purpose of these chapters. The intention is not to attain some kind of synthesis of the major contributions to the study of value in general, though such a synthesis has been envisaged by others. Najder (1975), for instance, noting the impossibility of presenting an adequate description of human individuals or groups in psychology, history, sociology, anthropology and economics without a statement of the individual or group's values, argued, 'This is why "value" should play the role of a basic concept integrating all disciplines concerned with man and his works' (p. 49). The difficulties of making this a practicable proposition in a way that both avoids vacuity and also faces the essential contestability[1] of many of the concepts involved appear daunting if not insuperable. Fortunately the aims of this chapter are more modest: to explore on a comparative basis some of the questions raised by our earlier discussion of social work and its values. Values are asserted with apparent ease, but are they easily articulated? It seems agreed that moral values are of central importance to social work, but can we readily understand what 'moral' means? Values have some connection with choice and decision. Can we see, from activities other than social work, what the connection might be?

The scope and substance of the following discussion is not readily summarised, but at this point it is appropriate to draw attention to various themes and ideas that enable us to take bearings as we cross, at speed, very varied territory, particularly since, as will soon be suggested, articulating even one's own 'values' is no straightforward task. As we review the four different sources of value-talk chosen (ordinary language, economics and sociology in this chapter, philosophy in the next) we will find that 'value' and 'values' do indeed perform a wide range of tasks. People explain the actions, usually of others or of other groups, in terms of particular 'values', as if there were a direct, almost causal connection; people are seen as imposing their values on others, though value judgments are often characterised as rather insubstantial; change in the course of a person's life and sometimes his actions are seen as the result of a value trade-off; and so on. So the terms 'value' and 'values' are worked hard and often, and they do important work (or, at the very least, important-sounding work). However, it is useful to distinguish between kinds of work, and some returns can be expected from distinctions between having or holding a value, making an evaluation and making a moral judgment. These distinctions cannot be rigidly applied, but they have the merit of indicating some ways in which 'values' can be unpacked.

None of these distinctions is simple, however. We may say of another that he holds or has a particular value on the basis of systematic observation, but the connection between behaviour and having a value is not a direct one. To say to myself 'I hold or have a particular value' seems to refer to at least three distinct, though connected, possibilities. To say, for instance, as social workers are often pictured as saying, 'I value democracy', may mean that I observe or try to observe rules of conduct that can be described as democratic. It can also mean that I see and accept democracy as an ideal form of political governance perhaps never to be fully realised, though particular political projects will be judged in terms of their approximation to the ideal. Again, it can refer to my pursuit of democratic purposes or my pursuing a way of life that could be called democratic. 'Making an evaluation' is not to be distinguished in the same way, though this notion also admits of distinction. Evaluations are made within a scheme of things or in situations involving some form of choice: they express a preference for X over Y or admiration (or the opposite) for X as a good (or bad) instance of a certain type of thing. They may also express an appreciation of something, for instance, as a good means of achieving a particular thing. Evaluations are best distinguished from value judgments by the latter's closeness to action. Value judgments may be of several distinct kinds, but one important grouping is that of moral judgments. Such judgments of what ought to be done overridingly in the light of human (or divine) considerations have been seen by moral philosophers as based on one of three foundations: duty, purpose or value.

'Value' and 'values' in ordinary language

It seems sensible to begin with 'value' and 'values' in ordinary language, since it could be expected that social work is particularly close to everyday affairs described in an ordinary manner.

At first sight it may appear an exaggeration to claim that 'value' and 'values' figure to any significant extent outside philosophy, economics and sociology, but once one is alerted to the possibility the frequency of reference in non-disciplinary contexts is remarkable. Over the last few weeks, for example, I have heard the following sentences in different kinds of relatively informal setting:

> I think A has a false set of values.
> B believes in getting value for money.
> What's the value of honesty, these days?
> We must just agree to differ: it's a question of values.
> His values have changed.
> I think human life is a supreme value.
> I think human life has intrinsic value.
> C's values are all wrong; that's his trouble.
> If you ask me, education boils down to the imposition of middle-class values.

This list could easily be extended, but it is sufficient as it stands to help us to see a number of important features of ordinary value-talk. First, uses vary in their complexity and in the extent to which they overlap with use in academic disciplines. 'Value for money' seems to refer to a satisfactory economic exchange: the consumer in return for costs incurred is economically satisfied or psychologically perhaps more than satisfied with the outcome of the exchange. 'Intrinsic value' refers to a judgment or recognition or a kind that requires no further justification: 'value' in this sense is a rock-bottom thing. Downie and Telfer (1980, pp. 6–7) suggest that this characteristic is conceptually crucial in talking about a person's values: someone may value his sports car highly, but it would be odd to count this amongst his values, not because of any supposed superficiality in the person but because a person's values are what he values for their own sake. We do, however, talk of instrumental values, and ordinary reference to 'intrinsic' value suggests this at least by implied contrast. 'Falsity', on the other hand, when applied to 'values' suggests that values, whatever else they may be, are the kind of thing of which it makes sense to claim they are true or false. Alternatively, it suggests that people are not always frank about the master purposes that in fact govern their lives.

Second, it is instructive to note the different activities that in ordinary conversation are connected with 'values', just as, as we have seen, the professional social work literature at least implicitly recognises the different things people want to do or are expected to do with 'values'. So, in ordinary conversation 'values', whatever they turn out to be, are spoken of as the kind of thing that can be 'imposed', 'changed', 'exchanged', 'judged' as true or false, right or wrong, 'recognised' as attached in some way to something ('life has intrinsic value') or as somehow residing in it ('human life is a supreme value').

Third, the question of social context is significant. I mean by this not that a detailed description is required of the situation of friend, neighbour or colleague from which the sentences have been abstracted before they can be understood. Rather I refer to a more general feature shared by most of these quotations: most are fairly obviously taken either from relatively serious discussions of an issue (connected with human life, for instance) or from relatively serious judgments about persons, who from one point of view are described as if 'values' were their most important quality (C's values are all wrong; *that's* his trouble').

The first and second features of this sample of 'ordinary' value-talk will be discussed further when they recur in later parts of this chapter, but some of the implications of the third feature (the relative seriousness of context) merit consideration at this point. Professionals in sociology, philosophy and so on, and students who have often been the subjects of empirical enquiry, find it relatively easy to use sentences containing 'value' and 'values' and somewhat easy to talk about such sentences, though, as we shall see, not in an agreed nor always a clear manner. Such ease obscures the common difficulty of knowing not so much the meaning of 'value' and 'values' as what values we hold, what valuations and value judgments we have in fact made, assumed, or even stated. The problem has been well expressed by Michael Oakeshott (1933), in the unlikely role of spokesman for the ordinary, unselfconscious individual. In discussing the common view that valuation is a form of feeling rather than of thought, Oakeshott argues that valuation is not feeling that in any sense precludes it from being thought:

Nevertheless, if by calling it feeling, it is intended to assert that valuation is often an elementary and unselfconscious form of thinking, no dispute is likely to arise. For most of us valuation is an almost unreflective process; many of our judgments of value are vague and inexplicit; often they must be inferred from our actions . . . for the most part our judgments of value are presented indirectly, in the form of actions and not of propositions; and we are rarely conscious of a continuous attempt to make our world of values coherent. (pp. 276–7)

This description of the difficulties of becoming aware of our valuations and judgments of value has serious implications for those who see self-awareness as a significant objective in the training of social workers and social policy practitioners. The objective of self-awareness is commonly set for social workers, though auto-biographical self-knowledge is more usually stressed than know-ledge of one's own values; but awareness of 'own values' is increas-ingly urged for those concerned with social policy. Thus, Madison (1980) has recently argued:

It is equally important for planners and decision-makers to be increasingly aware of their own values as they evolve them in the life-long process of clarifying their philosophy of life, the basis for values. This will help them guard against injecting their own values into policy, rather than shape it in the image of the choices that make up the general consensus. (p. 42)

However, for present purposes it is more important to pursue the implications of 'valuation' as a form of thought which can, on certain occasions, *become* explicit. The implications are practical and important if one is concerned with discovering what values a person or a group of people has. To discover this it is insufficient to address to them a question like 'What are your values?' This is rather like asking a senior civil servant 'What is your policy?' – not because one is in the realm of the indiscreet, but because of the problems of articulating any response at all. This does not mean that nothing a person says or can say in reply to the question is germane or that the question can be answered only by paying exclusive attention to how a person 'behaves'. It does mean that simple answers to 'What are your values' or 'Does *x* count amongst your values? cannot be taken at face value. Referring to one kind of value, moral value, Barnsley (1972) suggests the active social con-texts in which people may say something other than what first comes into their heads when asked a rather strange question about 'values' or 'valuations':

> our general knowledge of a particular society should also indicate to us the kind of contexts in which we would expect ethical discussion and advice to occur. Relating formal discussions given by leaders to their people, or by heads of organisations to their members, or by parents to their children often form examples of these. Situations of crisis, or at least of perceived moral dilemma, are another useful type of context. (p. 48)

Those subjected to annual soliloquies from heads of institutions may see situations of crisis as a more likely and a more lively source.

A crisis, it may be supposed, constitutes a kind of jolt and a pressure to express particular preferences. The sort of situation Barnsley probably had in mind can be illustrated from a speech by Truewit in Ben Jonson's play *Epicoene, or The Silent Woman*.

> Why, here's the man that can melt away his time, and never feels it! What between his mistress abroad and his ingle at home, high fare, soft lodgings, fine clothes, and his fiddle, he thinks the hours ha' no wings or the day no post horse. Well, sir gallant, were you strook with the plague this minute or condemned to any capital punishment tomorrow, you would begin then to think and value every article o' your time, esteem it at the true rate and give all for it.
>
> (Act 1, sc. 1)

This quotation from a playwright usually considered to have been in close touch with the ordinary London life of his time illustrates, as did the earlier sentence from non-professional conversation, the common usage of 'value'. Like them it suggests aspects important to those interested in value-talk in the more specialised field of social work, but, again like them, it does not enable us to settle in a definite way some of the problems implicit in common usage. Are we to say of the character to whom Truewit refers that before the plague or his sentence he had no sense of values, of priorities; that he had no values or that he valued equally kinds of pleasure between which he made little or no distinction? Once the plague or the sentence of capital punishment is admitted into his reality, are we to say he is making new evaluations or truly evaluating what he at last recognises as good? And for him it appears that what may be really good is that for which he would now exchange all, all seen previously perhaps as valued.

This comparatively brief look at 'value' and 'values' in ordinary conversation helps to illustrate the complex range of meanings and to demonstrate that value-talk is somewhat more problematic than is assumed by the social work writers whose work has been considered. However, as we have seen, ordinary reference to value and values overlaps with academic use, particularly in economics, sociology and philosophy, and the term reflects rather than resolves a range of difficulties. 'Values' are spoken of as if they were part of the actual furniture of the real world, as personal possessions or as part of the organic fabric of a society or of a personality. They cannot always be reached in or by argument, but they can in certain circumstances be judged or expressed in judgments. They are seen as either intrinsic or instrumental and as a blend (or confusion) of two different kinds of statements: those referring to what is the case and those referring to what ought to be or ought to be brought into being for a number of distinct reasons. 'Values' are often assumed to be only 'moral', but it is important to appreciate non-moral values. The statement 'His values are all wrong', for instance, can be construed in two ways: 'he adopts or has adopted a wrong set of moral principles', and 'his behaviour is unacceptable on moral or aesthetic or prudential grounds (or a combination of these)'.

The next sections in this and the following chapter are concerned with three disciplines in which the terms 'value' and 'values' play a significant part: economics, sociology and philosophy. It is not assumed that because the same words appear in each of these disciplines they necessarily share the same concepts. Indeed, it will become apparent that they are not dealing with different aspects of the same concept, but using the same term to stand for distinct concepts in three different fields of enquiry. It will also be evident that not only are there crucial theoretical differences concerning the explanation of value (in economics, for example, the contribution of labour to value has been differently assessed at different periods, and Marx's idea of surplus value has been heavily contested), but also (this applies particularly in sociology) the concept 'value' may have no agreed, settled place in the discipline. In the present enquiry these considerations may increase the difficulty of grasping any particular disciplinary treatment of 'value' and 'values', but they also constitute a positive encouragement to persevere. The treatment of values in disciplines other than social work is only comparatively more secure, and so social workers should not feel uniquely burdened with problems in this area nor be tempted to take over in a wholesale manner any one disciplinary treatment as a complete solution to the problems with social work values, acknowledged or not.

'Value' in economics

It may appear initially that the possibility of disciplinary restrictiveness – namely, that the consideration of value within any one discipline is of exclusive interest only to the practitioners of that discipline – is most strong in economics, where exchange-value, and value-in-use have been central notions from the beginnings of the subject. As Adam Smith wrote:

> The word value . . . has two different meanings, and sometimes expresses the utility of some particular object, and sometimes the power of purchasing other goods which the possession of that object conveys. The one may be called 'value in use'; the other 'value in exchange'. The things which have the greatest value in use have frequently little or no value in exchange; and, on the contrary those which have the greatest value in exchange have frequently little or no value in use. (1904, Book I, Chapter IV, p. 30)

(He cites water and diamonds respectively as examples.) However, it does seem that value-talk in general is often heavily influenced by the meaning of 'value' for the economist.

So Quay, in an article interestingly entitled 'Morality by Calculation of Values', argues that 'value' implies the possibility of exchange:

> So long as one object has as great effectiveness for the attainment of given ends as some other, it is of equal value with it or with anything else which is no more, no less effective in the same respect. Thus the commercial origins of the words in English are still evident; and 'values' never wholly sheds its denotation of a worth-for-exchange.

Quay is probably correct about the continuing actual influence of the commercial origins of the term, but we do not always have to credit such influence with legitimacy. Kant, for example, whose philosophy is taken by critics and supporters of traditional social work as central to the exposition of social work values, provides a warning. He argues against too easy a transposition from talk of the value of things or perhaps of situations to talk of the value of persons: to talk of the value of persons has to do with consideration of dignity rather than calculation of price.

However, such a warning should not be allowed to lend weight to the assumption that economics will necessarily provide misleading guidance for social workers, who, in some way or other, are concerned with altruism rather than what some have treated systematically as the selfish considerations of economics. Such an assumption derives in part from attempts to define the subject of social policy or social welfare as distinct from that of economic policy by categorising the former as the work of 'goodies' concerned with such ideals as social integration and the latter as the suspect work of those who were bent on individual satisfaction. It is a misleading assumption, not only because contemporary economists are beginning to turn their attention to 'unselfish economics' (just as they are beginning to study values that are described as without price), but because it contains an unwarranted view of the subject of economics. Downie (1980), for example, argues that 'It is not strictly accurate . . . to describe the economic relation as one of self-interest, or egoism' simply because each party attempts to maximise gain for himself: a person's conception of 'good' may include the realisation of the good of others. He suggests that a term preferable to 'self-interest' is one introduced in 1933 by Wickstead, namely 'non-tuism'. By this Wickstead makes the point that economic relations are not based on an exclusion from my mind of everyone except myself; they potentially include everyone except the other person involved in the exchange. Similarly, Lamont (1955) argues against characterising the economic relation, as distinct from the judicial relation and the relation of fellowship (and it is worth noting that the relationship of social worker and client is analysable into at least these three distinct relationships), as one in which the parties are egoists. Each party, in Lamont's view, is engaged in the pursuit of a total conception of good, using scarce resources, but the particular end pursued by each at any particular time is not also an end to the partner in the transaction. In anyone's total conception of good there will be some ends that are shared with others and some that are not. For Lamont there is no necessary assumption of egoism built into the idea or the reality of the economic relation – only the absence of the notion of or the attempt to achieve the good that is shared, the common good. Other kinds of relationship *are* concerned with the common good, of course, and our review of social work controversies indicated the different definitions of the common good advanced by the contestants.

'Value', as has been indicated, is a key concept in the study of economics, but it is not easily separated from a cluster of terms such as 'satisfaction', 'price', 'utility' and so on. Robinson (1964) in a chapter on the classical economists finds it difficult to pin 'value' down. It does not mean usefulness or 'the good that goods do us'. Nor is it the simple equivalent of price, though prices where they exist are often the best indicators of value that we have. As Sinden and Worrell (1979) argue, 'that is exactly what they [prices] are – indicators. They do not measure values; they indicate how people feel about the relative value of things they exchange with other people.' Generally speaking, it is perhaps best to take 'value' in economics as a property of objects and situations consisting of the capacity to satisfy. It is not a fixed, intrinsic property, since it is obvious that the same object or situation will have a different value at different times for different people.

> Value is a property of things, but a different kind of property from colour or weight. A flower is blue regardless of whether this makes any difference to anyone, but things only have value when their existence does make a difference to someone. The value of a thing derives basically from some need or desire which it has the capacity to satisfy. The greater this capacity the greater its value will usually be. (Sinden and Worrell, 1979)

This perspective has a number of important implications for the consideration of value and values. First, it is always worth (of some particular value) at least raising the question of any project, 'What is its value?' or 'How much satisfaction and of what kinds will be produced at the cost of what other satisfactions?' It is, of course, also important to ask a more sociological question concerning *whose* satisfactions. It is even worth raising the question in situations in which what is at issue can be described as a matter of inestimable worth (as in the case of a human life). This is not because 'unpriced' values are easily measured or because, even if they were, their calculation would settle the issue. Rather, in social work, which is often criticised as insufficiently cost-conscious, it is important to appreciate the extent of costs which are the postponement or the neglect of the realisation of situations valued by other people.

Second, economic discussion of 'value' emphasises the role of human activity in relation to 'goods' and 'commodities'. Baier (in Baier and Rescher (eds), 1969), in one of the few attempts to establish a groundwork for the general study of value, argues that 'economists draw the indispensable distinction (largely lost to sociologists) between, on the one hand, the *value* of things, and on the other, the values of individuals or societies'. This distinction is important, but it is crucial not to overlook the relations between objects and people, individually or in groups. Admittedly, in social welfare talk, the notion of commodities or 'goods' seems to fit badly at least with some of the usually acknowledged values: self-determination, for example, cannot easily be seen as the right to a commodity, let alone as a commodity. Yet in economic discussions the role of human activity and also the complexity of the activity of valuing receive an emphasis that has implications for any general consideration of value.

In economics the 'valuer' may be seen as a socially abstracted and highly cost-conscious individual or as much more closely connected to 'society', but however he is viewed the activity of 'valuing' is seen as complex. The 'valuer' is not like a bishop bestowing a simple blessing on an undifferentiated flock which thereby becomes a blessed (or valued) group: he may make calculations and judgments but he certainly *chooses*. The French economist Turgot argued that the *valure estimative* of a good was formed by judgment of a number of factors, including the ease with which it could be obtained, its scarcity, its ability to satisfy a want, and so on. Nor does the valuation inevitably create value; sometimes in economic thought value is recognised but in an 'exaggerated' manner (as in an expensive French Impressionist painting).

Third, we can use the work of economists to interpret the idea of value judgment in a particular way, and this idea must occupy an important role in any attempt to come to terms with 'value' and 'values'. It can most happily be illustrated through the treatment of 'value judgment' by a philosopher, Lamont (1955), both because this conveys a clear idea of the kind of judgment this is and also because it indicates that value judgments are not the exclusive concern of any of the disciplines we are considering. Economists commonly eschew value judgments, unless these are of a universally accepted kind (Sugden, 1982, chapter 1), but what Lamont calls the comparative value judgment seems to be at the heart of economics.

Lamont argues for a strong distinction between what he calls the comparative value judgments (in contrast to the simple positive value judgments, 'x is good') and a number of other judgments often taken to be value judgments. Thus, he is concerned to distinguish the comparative value judgments from moral judgments, judgments of efficiency and aesthetic judgments.

> Valuation or choice is concerned with the correlation of ends within a total *personal* conception of 'the good'. The moral judgment, on the other hand, being the assertion of a duty or obligation (or at least of something to which the notion of obligation is always relevant), always carries a reference to the conception of 'right' and therefore to an *inter-personal* order. The former is what may be called, for convenience, an 'economic' assessment of modes of action, while the latter is a 'juridical' assessment. (p. 11)

The simply positive value judgment indicates 'a state of affairs which the judger has a disposition to bring into existence, maintain in existence, allow to go out of existence or destroy' (p. 18), whereas the comparative value judgment estimates degrees of goodness amongst a group of things all regarded as good. 'The comparative value judgment is an expression of "choice" when objective circumstances . . . enforce on us the disagreeable necessity of renouncing one thing if the other is to be attained.' This disagreeable necessity is of considerable significance in the more general consideration of value and values. A valued project may have to be foregone in order to establish a more valued situation; norms that are judged appropriate to any one situation may clash; purposes within such a general thing as a way of life are not always at any given moment realisable or even compatible. Choice of these kinds is sometimes not much in evidence when we are offered a finite list of values. It is as if these were at all times compatible, on all occasions realisable or equally appropriate or made always equivalent demands.

'Value' and 'values' in sociology

'Value' and 'values' figure largely in sociological writing, but it must be acknowledged that they also figure somewhat loosely. In sociology 'value' and 'values' have been taken as that which satisfied motivation, as anything capable of being wished for, as any object of any need, as what people say they want, as the most general statements of legitimate ends which guide social action, as constituent facts of the social structure, and so on. Baier (in Baier and Rescher (eds), 1969), in search of a basis on which to clarify the concept of value, concluded that 'sociologists employ a bewildering profusion of terms, ranging from what a person wants, desires, needs, enjoys, prefers, through what he thinks desirable, preferable, rewarding, obligatory to what the community enjoins, sanctions or enforces' (p. 35). Hutcheon (1972), arguing towards a conceptual clarification of 'value' in sociological thought, has identified the following main ways in which sociologists have used the term: as objective group norms; as symbolising cultural ideals; as assessments of action (as, for example, in work which defines values solely in terms of the structure of occupational rewards); as beliefs of an effective or cognitive kind; as objects or an inherent aspect of objects (Hutcheon observes in this connection that Becker's view that all objects experienced by an individual becomes values for him 'would seem to render the term completely powerless as an ordering concept'); as essentially orientation, though the term 'value orientation' is often confusingly interchanged with attitude; and, finally, as generalised attitudes. In the light of such a rich variety of meanings, it is perhaps not surprising that in a recent monograph on the nature of sociology Harris (1980) can state that the term 'value' is 'currently unfashionable', though in his view it 'stands as an index of a number of interesting and important problems which may one day receive the attention they deserve' (p. 127).

However, it would be an extreme response to dismiss, as Baier does, the usefulness of the existing treatment of 'value' and 'values' by sociologists. The range of meaning or at least a significant section in sociological treatment is reflected in ordinary uses; people refer to different kinds of things as values and use the term to perform different tasks. More importantly, sociological use of the term raises very significant questions concerning the exploratory power of 'values' and the nature of values, not in the sense that an individual holds certain values, but in terms of the meaning and function of group or social values. Thus, sociologists refer to subcultural values; delinquency, for example, has been explained in terms of the direct expression in subcultural form of the submerged or implicit values of the wider society, such as excitement, hazarding and so on.

'Values' are also used in sociology to explain social cohesion and the continuity of groups. So, it is assumed, what holds institutional practices together is an explict or an implicit agreement, a value consensus, and the existence and continuation of a collectivity is good evidence for a continuing and an integrated system of values. Such assumptions have recently been stringently criticised in a book (Abercrombie *et al*, 1980) which draws attention to similarities between the dominant ideology thesis maintained by some Marxists and a Parsonian emphasis on the idea and the reality of the common culture.

> Both the Marxist dominant ideology theorists and their sociological counterparts make assumptions that are often unexamined. For example, the relation between dominant ideology and the dominant classes is not considered, the apparatus for the transmission of ideology and values is not investigated in detail, and incorporation via ideology or integration by shared values is all too often taken for granted once the existence of a dominant ideology or value system is demonstrated. (p. 158)

Now such considerations, interesting on a grand scale, may seem to be far removed from the values of social work. However, the general criticisms made by the authors can be directly applied on the small scale to the professional collectivity to raise questions about the existence and the function of shared values. It is simply an assumption that values are shared by social workers, though this is not a simple assumption, since it helps to establish the professional status of the occupation. It is also an assumption that the values in so far as they are shared actually further or are responsible for the cohesion of the collectivity: this must depend at least on the kind of values they are and the kind of 'thing' we take values to be.

Finally, sociological use raises another question concerning not the function of the values but the extent to which any grouping of values constitutes a system. Sociologists refer, for example, to particular groupings as 'typically capitalist' or as 'liberal', 'conservative' and so on. Identifying a number of values (and associated beliefs) in this way asserts that they cohere in a systematic manner precisely as ideas that are capitalist, liberal, conservative and so on. It is arguable that insufficient work is done before this identification, that values are grouped in a seemingly casual way, and that two or three central theorists are often taken as representative of a whole tradition. Nonetheless, the attempt to see a system of values and to judge what constitutes the system indicates lessons useful for the more general appreciation of 'value' and 'values', and, in particular, for 'social work values', where the fact and the principle of coherence are not immediately obvious.

7

Values, valuations and value judgments II

. . . falling in love is an appreciation of values: it is a conversion of facts into values.

J. Dowling, 'Conscience, love and doctrine'

Some personalities are steadier and tougher than others, less fluctuating in their valuations. . . . Night valuations differ from day valuations.

J.A. Hobson (1929), p. 53

Introduction

Philosophical work bearing on values, valuations and value judgments or on other 'distinguishable elements to which the word "value" is applied' (Hobson, 1929) is very extensive indeed. Even though this chapter is concerned with particular problems that have emerged in the course of the treatment of social work values earlier in this book, it will be possible to offer only a brief outline of some helpful themes and arguments that have emerged in philosophical discussion. Amongst these problems the most important are: the meaning of 'moral' in moral principle, moral value and so on; possible distinctions in value-talk as in possible differentiation between valuing as an experience and as a judgment; and how, if at all, argument about values is possible rather than shrugging the shoulders and moving on to the next piece of business. These questions are not easily posed, let alone answered, but some exploration of the contestable concepts involved is essential if we are to arrive at a better understanding of social work values.

The meaning of 'moral'

We all use the term 'moral' and many use it frequently, though it is not easy to pin down. Ossowska (1971), for instance, considers it an ambiguous term: it is used in opposition to 'physical', as in moral pain or humiliation as opposed to the hurt sustained in an accident; 'moral' is opposed to 'immoral' in what she calls a laudatory and hence emotionally loaded term; it is used to refer to sexual 'good' behaviour; it can be seen as equivalent to a tendency to improve, as in the idea of a moral tale; it can refer to a class of phenomena such as moral valuations as opposed to aesthetic appraisals. Some of these possible meanings are not of major importance, nor do they all have such serious implication once the meaning has been pointed out, but, as Downie and Telfer stated in a recent introduction to the philosophy of caring and curing, 'moral' remains 'a very slippery term indeed' (1980, p. 8). However, a beginning can be made by suggesting that 'moral' in moral principles, moral values, moral consideration, etc., has to do with that which is taken to be overriding. So, Stutchbury (1973) argues in connection with principles that 'One ought to describe those principles and those principles only which a person usually backs against all comers as his moral principles' (p. 110). Similarly, Margolis (1971) sees moral considerations as those overriding considerations which bear on the conduct of one's own life and the lives of others as such. For Margolis any consideration or 'any judgment or decision or policy is morally significant if it is concerned with the treatment of any form of life . . . in terms of relations, conditions, and the like that are thought, by the agents involved, to be preferable over all alternatives, for all living creatures considered' (p. 7).

This notion of 'overridingness' in terms of human concern takes us some way towards understanding 'moral', but there are different views on the reasons why the principles, considerations, etc., that are moral are overriding: they do not just happen to carry this special emphasis, nor do actors simply settle such questions by, as it were, using a set of already marked weights. The reasons given by philosophers are usually classified in general terms as deontological, or concerned with meeting obligations as such; teleological, or concerned with the achieving of purposes or goals; and axiological, or 'a type of moral theory based on values, as approved and disapproved, however this is judged, from *axion*, "what is worthy" ' (Emmet, 1979, p. 5). It is appropriate to illustrate these views in a little more detail, partly because at different stages social work has been influenced by the then dominant notions of morality – the idea of obligation and of the achievement of individual and social purposes was, as we have seen, a theme in the work of the Charity Organisation Society. Also philosophers have strongly argued that one and only one of the three conceptions could serve as the basis of morality: to be moral was to be concerned with such purposes as achieving the greatest happiness of the greatest number, *or* to be concerned only with meeting obligations because this was what was due or owing and not because by so doing one achieved some good or purpose, *or* to recognise that which is ultimately worthwhile. The following illustrations of the possible orientations will help to show what may be involved in 'moral'.

The overriding nature of duty as such, performing an act precisely because it is correctly described as one's duty, no longer holds sway, but it can be discussed through a recent attempt by Weston (1975) to criticise the dominant role now given to goals and the means to goals in writing on morality. Weston is interested in the subject of moral change and development (an aspect usually overlooked in social work) and in 'the moral notions contained in the first person judgment'. Each of these has implications for social workers interested in change of various kinds and as concerned with their own behaviour as with judgments clients might make of *their* own behaviour. Weston (1975), using extensive illustrations from the novels of Conrad, argues that morality is best approached through thinking of fidelity or the recognition of what is due to the significance certain features of a situation come to have for particular people:

> Moral notions I have suggested mark, not something which can assume an importance for a man, but *a kind of importance* which certain facts can have for him. It is this which is lost in asking 'why should one be moral?', for any answer to this must show how moral considerations are *given* importance rather than the kind of importance they embody. (p. 90); second italics added)

In this perspective morality does not have to do with doing right because one has a valued conception of oneself as the kind of person who goes about doing what is right or good. Nor is it concerned with the results to be expected from behaving in ways that count as those of friendship or count as charitable. Rather, moral considerations provide a 'limit' of some kind to what a man sees himself as doing. 'This', concludes Weston,

> directs us to consider the ways in which moral considerations
> can over-ride and provide a new perspective on purposive ones.
> And this points to . . . the nature of the importance moral
> considerations can have for a man, namely the way the notion of
> the self, and therefore of a man's life, is connected with that of
> morality. The deepest difference between purposive and moral
> ideas will appear in this. (p. 93)

The notion of a 'man's life' considered as a whole, figured, as we saw, in some of the theorising of the COS.

Other philosophers, of course, have strongly denied the difference between purposive ideas and moral ideas: for them it is not that morality could simply not be considered outside human purposes, but that morality was constituted in the following of an overriding human purpose. This, the teleological approach, has been usefully divided into two kinds by Emmet. In *The Moral Prism* (1979), the central argument of which I shall use shortly, Emmet distinguishes between two kinds of teleology. Teleology A, in which the end is specific and the means solely instrumental, is different in significant respects from teleology B, or a kind of purposive activity where the manner of achieving one's ends is not simply of significance but is somehow an actual part of the purposive activity. Roughly speaking, she suggests, the second kind of teleology might be called the pursuit of a life-style. However, 'There are life-styles and life-styles', and Emmet suggests some criteria by which a life-style could count as moral. It should be 'serious' or carry commitments (and, as we have seen in Chapter 1, commitment is not primarily a sense of feeling or of being rather generally engaged, but has to do with an attitude towards specifiable beliefs); it should 'include considerations as to what one thinks it important to do and in what ways; how to conduct one's relations with other people; and being aware and prepared to be critical of one's basic approvals and disapprovals'. These criteria are mentioned not simply as a way of exploring further the idea of a style of life, but also because, as was noted in Chapter 1, social work or rather the profession of social work has, at certain times in the history of social work, been described as a way of life. What those who so described it had in mind was not some reference to style of living but certain key moral considerations that governed one's working *and* non-working life, certain considerations which made of the different activities in a life a whole valued as such. Whether social work could alone bear the weight of this is another matter.

The primacy of value in morality is, as we have seen, asserted by those described as axiologists. The term 'axiology' was introduced into philosophical discussion by Urban at the beginning of the present century in what Findlay (1970) describes with rather daunting approval as a 'heavily excellent book'. Axiologists sought to explore ultimately worthwhile things (as well as those that were counter-worthwhile) and worthwhileness and counter-worthwhileness in general. What ought to be done bore a close relationship, not to achieving certain goals nor to doing what is duly required because it is due, but to doing what is judged excellent or worthy. Valuation is seen as of prime importance, and is recognised as being necessarily consequent on some character which can be distinguished from the value we may find in an object: we value objects and we value them for certain attributes or under certain specifications. 'Even when individuals are valued for being the individuals they are, there is an obscure reference to specifications they fulfill, and occasions on which those specifications are manifest' (Findlay, 1970, p. 7). The early axiologists, including Brentano, Meinong, Rashdall and Scheler, now seem somewhat distant, but a recent attempt to ground morality in caring for and about others as estimable and to be esteemed can be used to illustrate the general axiological perspective. It has the additional advantage that caring is clearly an important aspect of social work and that an account of social work that is adequate must include some account of it.

Beehler (1978) argues against those like Hare (1952) who believe that I am justified in asserting 'You ought to do x, if and only if I have adopted the principle that x-ing is in general good.' Beehler states that addressing an 'ought' statement, so understood, to someone, could not actually accomplish anything:

If all that is required to entitle one to address 'ought' – statements to others is one's own unilateral subscription to a principle of discrimination, the question arises why such statements should ever have an effect.

He also argues against a position which in his view marks an improvement on Hare's, namely that of Phillips and Mounce (1970). According to the latter I am justified in saying 'You ought to do so' through an established rule which members of the community accept: the utterance has the implication that the person to whom it is addressed already has a reason for carrying out what it says and this reason is an established rule. There is an important relation between the person to whom an 'ought' statement is addressed and the rule the judgment appeals to, though the person has not decided on the rule. Phillips and Mounce argue that it is not the case that we have *decided* that generosity is a virtue, or that lying is wrong. Beehler, on the contrary, argues that we have decided that lying is wrong, etc., but what we have not decided is that it should matter to us that lies are not told. He seeks what is given not in the rules of language, as Phillips and Mounce do, but in forms of life:

And the form of life which is the foundation of morality is: caring about others. The answer to the one who asks why lies ought not to be told or promises broken, is not – 'This language game is played'. The answer is, because pain will be given. (p. 17)

So far I have tried simply and briefly to illustrate the three main types of ethical theorising, which centre respectively on one of three distinctive terms: principle, purpose, and approval as worthwhile or excellent. I have also indicated where appropriate any particular connection with thinking about social work. I have not offered any sustained criticism, mainly because Emmet (1979) has recently argued for an inclusive view of morality which emphasises activity or practice and adopts principle, *and* purpose, *and* approval, as worthwhile or excellent:

Morality is not so much an activity in itself as on the back of other activities, concerned with what one does in them, and how and when. The particular feature in morality dominant at any given time will be likely to be that most characteristically associated with whatever activity we are involved in. In acting politically, the feature of purpose will be dominant, in acting in a legal or administrative capacity the emphasis will be on principles to be applied impartially. But other factors within morality may become relevant both to the occasion and manner of what is done; there are times when a purpose in politics may be challenged for a principle, and times when sympathetic discretion will temper judicial impartiality and times in personal relations when keen-edged criticism is more appropriate than tolerant acceptance.

It will perhaps not be surprising if this moral eclecticism appeals to social workers, though there is nothing easy in Emmet's view that reasons have to be shown for adopting different stances at different times. However, it is a view that deserves most careful consideration as an adequate reflection of the complexities of moral thought and a full recognition of the complexity of situations in which a moral position is asserted and explored or a moral rule involved.

Some distinctions in talk of 'value' and 'values'

I want to look at distinctions drawn between different senses of 'value' and then to consider distinctions drawn between different activities, such as holding a value, evaluating, judging. I also wish to consider one crucial distinction drawn or discussed by many writers, namely that between 'is' statements and 'value' statements.

The most clear and useful distinctions between ways in which the term 'value' is commonly used have been drawn by Charles Morris (1956), to whom reference has already been made. He refers to 'operative values', 'conceived values' and 'object values'. Operative values arise from the actual direction of behaviour expressing preference or repeated choice. Morris gives as an illustration the case of a person shown a series of pairs of pictures and asked to select his preference within each pair. At the end of the session the selected paintings are examined, and it turns out that they have in common a number of features which distinguish them from the paintings that had not been preferred. It may then be said that the person values paintings with contrasting colours, for instance, and perhaps that he values contrasts. In this type of situation 'value' refers to what as a matter of fact accounts for the preference (contrasts, in the example) and also to what in fact turns out to be preferred (paintings with contrasting colours).

'Value' in the second of the senses identified by Morris refers to objects or situations *conceived* as preferable. In this sense of 'value', behaviour that expresses preference may be directed by the anticipation of the outcome of such behaviour. Morris uses the well-known definition of Kluckhohn *et al*. (1951) (which is the definition most used in social work discussion) to illustrate conceived values:

> Value is more than mere preference; it is limited to those types of preferential behaviour based upon conceptions of the desirable which influences the selection from available modes, means, and ends of action.

It is perhaps not clear why preferences should be characterised as 'mere' (*some* casual preferences may be), but what is significant in this use of 'value' is a conception of what is desirable and not an observer-based report on what actually turns out to be the discriminating 'value', together with the idea that the conception of what is desirable actually influences the conscious selection of one mode, means or ends amongst all the possible modes, means and ends.

Finally, 'object values' refer not to what turns out to be what is actually preferred, nor to anyone's conception of what is preferable in the available world, but to what is to be preferred. In this sense of 'value' it is the equivalent of that which *is* desirable, whether or not it is in fact preferred or is conceived as preferable by this or that individual or group.

A different but possibly more generally useful three-fold classification is offered by Najder (1975) in a discussion of the ambiguity of the term 'value'. Najder distinguishes quantitative value, attributive value, and underlying or axiological value. Quantitative value is what something is worth and is expressed in some unit of measurement or of comparison. Najder suggests as an instance of value in this sense the following questions: 'What is the value of this house?' 'What is the value of a mother's life compared to the life of her child?'; 'What is the value of *Four Quartets* in the corpus of T.S. Eliot?' These are all questions that can be posed without absurdity, but they do not all seem to indicate worth as expressed in *units* of measurements: an answer to the second question is scarcely possible in terms of such units, though it is possible to consider the question in terms of priorities in situations of limited resources. Attributive value refers to a thing or property to which value is ascribed: a man's actions can be said to possess considerable social value. Axiological value is defined by Najder as an idea that makes us consider a given object, quality or event valuable: the value of life consists in living with human dignity. The two distinct notions of *attributing* value and *recognising* value are of general importance to any discussion of 'value' and 'values'.

Distinctions have also been developed between the actual experience of valuing something or somebody and the act of evaluation as reasoning concluding in evaluative judgments. Najder, for example, cites the instance of remembering friends in value-laden terms and suggests that such experiences as admiration should be seen as essentially evaluative experiences. Berleant (1973) makes the same kind of distinction, though he suggests that the actual experience of valuing something is harder to pin down. He sees the failure to observe the distinction as having important implications:

> our difficulties in dealing with values follow from the failure to distinguish clearly and effectively between values as characteristic kinds of human experiences and value judgments as statements about such kinds of experiences. The first are the actual occasions of valuing themselves and, like all direct and immediate experience, are non-cognitive. Value judgments, on the other hand . . . are framed about our value experiences; they offer a conceptual formulation or ordering of the valuational mode of experience . . . such statements can be verified by placing them against the value experiences of men, and consequently these statements take on a cognitive character.

Later, Berleant distinguishes valuation as the direct experience of valuing, and evaluation as the reflection on that experience, and my preference would be not to use 'value judgment' to make that distinction since Berleant's use of the term does not appear to recognise that value judgments characteristically carry implications for action and for reasons for action as well as for enjoyment or contemplation. However, what matters – to use the example of friendship again – are distinctions between the experiences of nurturing friends, cherishing the idea and ideal of friendship, remembering people as friends, and recognising an obligation as due to friendship.

Not all value judgments are moral judgments, though, as has already been noted, this sometimes seems to be assumed in social welfare discussions; nor are all moral judgments, judgments of value. Failure to draw the necessary distinctions partly derives from the fact that, as Quinton (1973) has noted, all forms of value judgment share a basic vocabulary: ' "good", "bad", "right", "wrong", "ought", and "ought not" occur in counsels of prudence, technical prescriptions and critical judgments as ineliminably as they do in moral injunctions'. He goes on to indicate a brief but useful differentiation between value judgments of different kinds:

> A material criterion of morality would be that a value judgment is moral if it evaluates actions in the light or their bearing on the satisfaction of the agent; technical if the evaluating factor is the minimisation of time and cost; aesthetic if it is the reward of satisfaction available in the long run to a contemplative spectator, and so on. (p. 380)

The relationship between statements of fact and statements of obligation, or the 'is–ought' debate, has a long history in philosophy to which nothing approaching justice can be done in the present work; but the question cannot be ignored. Two considerations seem to be crucial, in view of the common assumption in social work that any observation is so saturated with a person's values, personal and political, that the most serious question to ask of anyone concerns not their beliefs as to matters of fact but their ideology, i.e. the ways in which they seek to confront others about that on which they themselves stand in no need of argument. First, how can statements about what is the case be distinguished from recommendations in relation to future actions? Second, having distinguished two kinds of statement, what kinds of relationship should be considered between the two? It seems to be assumed in discussion of 'value-free' activity, whether the practice in question is that of sociology or of social work, that because descriptive statements are related in very interesting and perhaps complex ways to normative statements about what ought to be done, it is not possible or it is pointless to attempt to separate the two: in the end, and for that matter in the beginning, *all* is value or ideology or whatever.

One way of making the distinction between 'is' and 'ought' statements is to consider the difference between factual beliefs and values. Values, however they are understood, always entail some beliefs about what is the case: values as norms or rules entail beliefs about the real world to which they apply – a rule in a vacuum is simply not a rule: similarly values as purposes and values as ideals are connected in some way to beliefs about what there is that has to be overcome or changed. Factual beliefs, on the other hand, do not necessarily entail values. Beliefs concern what is true; values constitute or may constitute various reasons for action. Beliefs of a factual nature rely on evidence in a way that values do not. Williams (1973) has identified two senses in which this key notion of reliance on evidence holds. In a weak sense the content of a given belief can be supported by certain evidential propositions. In a stronger sense a man may say he has the belief in question *because* he has the particular evidence: if he ceased to believe the evidence he would cease to have the belief.

This general distinction between factual belief and value is relatively clear, but in the practical world we seem often to be moving beyond the belief that something is the case or the assertion that it is at least *towards* what appear to be judgments involving values. We say, for example, that a report shows a good piece of social work, that it is a clear case of emotional deprivation or that the situation in locality is clearly one of urban or social deprivation. Yet such judgments should be understood as still firmly in the factual realm. A distinction developed by Margolis (1971) between 'findings' and 'appreciative judgments' may help to develop this point.

Margolis argues that what he calls appreciative judgments depend logically on taste or personal conviction or personal preference, whereas findings behave in the same way as factual judgments. By this he means that the truth of findings can be tested on recognisably public grounds; findings that are logically contradictory cannot both be true, and findings confirmed as true state what is the case. He illustrates his view of what findings are by referring to professional practice. Thus, it is a medical finding that a particular person has cancer; it is a legal finding that a particular person murdered another and so on. A similar distinction drawn by Fallding (1968), one of the few sociologists who has written helpfully on the subject of values, helps us to see what is at issue. He has called attention to 'a class of intellectual judgments that are judgments of value in the purely intellectual sense of judgment'. Judgments in this particular category

> simply make the observation that, in terms of its nature,
> something is good or bad, and they do not add anything by way
> of personal preference or exhortation to others to side for or

against the phenomenon reported. You can use your intellect to judge whether a cabbage, a lung, a piano, a bridge, a surgeon, a marriage, or a constitution is good or bad, and still leave entirely unsaid what attitude you mean to take to the fact. If a line is to be drawn in discussions about value it is here. (p. 73)

A line does require to be drawn between statements of fact and expressions of value, and it must be accepted that no obligation or preference can logically be deduced from merely factual statements. However, there are two important ways in which 'fact' and 'value' at least begin to merge, even though the latter cannot be related to the former in terms of deduction. First, we meet in social welfare a number of terms which incorporate factual and value-laden features inseparably interwoven. Terms like 'harm' or 'human harm' both describe a situation in a factual way (it is harmful) and at the same time indicate that it ought to be avoided or compensated for, or at least that its realisation ought not actually to be pursued. Second, whilst the distinction between an 'ought' judgment and a description of mere fact is clear, it is important to note that the facts, particularly those of a social situation, are frequently something more than 'mere'. The facts of a situation are not an array of neutral substances over which an 'ought' blessing of some kind is then separately intoned. The facts are often facts of an institutional nature into which obligatoriness of some kind has been inserted, is present as part of that situation seen from a particular point of view. As Emmet (1958) has argued, the facts of social situations become facts 'because they are seen within the context of ways in which people live together, and the common values these involve. And anyone who responsibly accepts such a way of living accepts its commitments.'

Argument about values

It is possible to use 'value' and 'values' as conversation-terminators. An illustration of such a use was one of the examples of value-talk taken from ordinary conversation which we looked at earlier: 'We must just agree to differ: it's a question of values.' Such an approach is actually encouraged by a variety of views on the meaning and function of judgments of value: that they simply and only report or express people's attitudes for or against something; that 'values' are the fancy clothes in which we dress our egotistical or our materialistic interests; that 'values' are at the root of social disputes, but they can only be fought over by a kind of proxy, and never battled through to an exchange of ideas and a conversion or change of mind or even a conversation. Against the views that more or less conspire to shorten or to trivialise our response to a person's statement of his values or to his making or reporting a value judgment or a valuation it is important, as Brown (1976) has argued, to make 'at least a little room for rational criticism' between dogmatism and scepticism.

Brown starts from the position that it is unsatisfactory that rationality should be excluded from discourse that is evaluative and confined strictly to the sphere of the descriptive. He suggests that the use of two principles will enable us to see how value judgments ('appraisals of such things as scenery, a person's character, works of art etc.') can be rationally considered and debated. These principles are that criticism need not be justificatory, and that making a value judgment is a matter of taking up an attitude of a special kind, namely an attitude on behalf of all. The second is basically a description of a rejection procedure: maintaining an attitude on behalf of all entails the attempt to find instances of rejection, to find people who do not have the attitude in question. 'If, despite all attempts to find grounds for rejecting it, a value judgment has so far survived criticism, it may be tentatively accepted; but this does not render it exempt from further criticism.' It is not sufficient, however, for a dissenting attitude statement simply to be made for the value judgment as such to fall immediately. 'Instead it may lead to a discussion the outcome of which could be the sustaining of the judgment through a change in the dissenter's attitude, or rejection of the judgment, or even the endorsement of a new judgment incorporating the previously dissenting attitude.'

This represents one attempt in relation to one kind of value judgment to show the role of rational discourse. It can be used to illustrate that rationality can have no place at all if 'values' and 'value' evaluations and value judgments are considered together as an indivisible kind of heavenly *lumpen*, or if one adopts the attitude 'My values, right or wrong, but *mine*.' *Rational* considerations lead to the making and the marking of distinctions, and it is only within the different categories and in their distinctive relationships that rational discourse can proceed. Factual beliefs should be distinguished from 'values', beliefs held against the very idea of contrary evidence (counter-factual beliefs) should be distinguished from value judgments and from the rules of intelligible action that help to constitute a form of social living. If these and other distinctions are observed then we can reason with each other about our ideals (is X such that Y's idolisation of X is justified), about rules of different kinds, and about purposes entertained as human. Ultimately, we may have to accept the position outlined in the sentence from ordinary conversation already quoted: 'We must just agree to differ', but we do not have to start with the ultimate, and an *agreement* to differ is much more than a shrug or the expression of a feeling. It may constitute knowledge and understanding of the extent and the nature of the difference from others.

8

Conclusions

'Social work values' cannot be grasped and considered within professional boundaries alone. This enquiry has proceeded in part by attempting to consider in depth existing statements about social work values, but also by ranging broadly in the fields of other disciplines or of no discipline in particular. The enquiry has, however, to come to some conclusions other than those simply involving the inherent complexity of the topic or listing the errors of previous explorers. The conclusions are of two different but connected kinds. First, at a formal level I attend to the distinguishable elements within value-talk. Second, I turn to issues of coherence, context and substance. Becoming clear about the elements is not any negligible accomplishment; it has the importance of scaffolding in relation to a building. Or, to change the metaphor, distinguishing between those elements that are distinguishable helps to clarify the euphoric mists which surround value-talk in social work – and in other activities. This, however, does not in itself establish the issues around which 'values' in social work or elsewhere may cohere. The final stage in the argument of this book is that social work values cohere in the notion of a practice and of the practical mode of experience. Such a notion supplies the necessary coherence and also context.

The distinguishable elements distinguished

1 Some ways of talking suggest that 'values' are a kind of real object, but a less misleading approach is to consider people behaving in particular ways or choosing to do certain kinds of things. It is people

138

who hold values, treat things as being of value, make different kinds of judgments of value. In developing our grasp of 'value' and 'values' it is preferable to go for verbs rather than nouns. In the preceding discussions only a small number of verbs has been considered: 'holding', 'valuing', 'evaluating', 'judging'. There are obviously very many others: 'commending', 'loving', 'being concerned for', 'caring for', 'redeeming', and so on. No single action-word can give the key. 'Value' and 'values' refer to people pursuing a range of objectives, and undertaking a wide variety of tasks.

2 To say someone has or holds a value is to draw attention to relatively settled features of their situation, though these features are subject to change. To say someone has or holds a value may refer to the norms and rules they use in the business of living or to the ideals they cherish which may penetrate their way of doing things or even express in a very summary form a manner of life. Again 'holding a value' may refer to beliefs of a particular kind, counter-factual as opposed to factual beliefs or to purposes or goals. Talk of a person's values *tout court* conveys very little: we need to have more precise reference.

3 We do, of course, speak frequently of the value of things, of the value of a quality. So, it could be said that certain psychologists have stressed the positive aspects of human aggression or that they have investigated the value it has, though it would be strange to say that aggression was one of their values. However, to speak of the value of aggression is to refer to the role it plays within a wider, purposive scheme of things; for example, within life as the realisation of ambition or as the continuity of the species.

4 When we speak of people valuing things we refer to their forming a quantitive assessment or valuation, with the ideas of exchange and of comparison somewhere in the background. We also refer to the ways in which they behave towards objects, situations and people: they show that and to what degree they appreciate the object, situation or person. Valuing may also refer to behaviour towards an object *as* foreshowing certain appreciated features: an object may have sentimental value. We also speak of evaluating an object, person or situation: we may rank or grade something as an *x* and as an *x* of a certain kind. For instance, we rank or grade undergraduate work as a first class and even as a 'good' first. In doing this we place ourselves in the position of answering questions, if required, about what its goodness consists in and also what kind of

goodness. Such questions are answered, according to Midgley (1978), not in terms of additional facts somehow piled on top of those we already have, but in terms of a specification: the goodness and the kind of goodness is in the facts seen in this way, from that point of view.

5 Value judgments express approval or disapproval of some kind in the light of action. One type of value judgment has been given emphasis in the foregoing discussion, namely moral judgments. Moral judgments relate to actions that ought to be performed (or shunned) because of overriding considerations of duty or principle, of purpose and of value. These judgments and other value judgments share a common description: they are statements of a particular kind, statements that express the result of the activity of judging. So, value judgments are capable of some reasoning: they are not simple reports, they have a place in a wider scheme of things.

6 Just as it is sometimes implied that 'values' occupy space in the real world, so it can be assumed that 'values' occupy the total available space: values saturate the world, and once one has grasped the values of a group or a person one has understood their most important aspect. This assumption is sometimes accompanied by another, that values cannot be systematically discussed or rationally argued through. The preceding sections indicate that rational argument is feasible and necessary if only to establish the different uses of 'value' and 'values'. 'Values' must be separated from factual beliefs, and these in turn should be distinguished from counter-factual beliefs. This does not, of course, mean that 'fact' and 'value' can always in every case be separated, nor that complex relations may not bring into connection in certain cases 'fact' and 'value'. Intelligibility is different from desirability, worthwhileness or what is considered fitting.

7 Statements about what values people hold, what valuations or what value judgments they make, can be in the first, second or third person, singular or plural, but there are certain problems in describing the situation from someone else's point of view. Reports of the values other people hold are often based on their behaviour, but inferences from choice to a person's valuation system cannot always be reliably made. Weale (1979) has drawn attention, for example, to the simplest case of difficulty, namely indifference. Indifference has a place in everyone's system of valuation, except perhaps for the hysteric, but it is difficult to assess from the outside: either an

alternative is chosen and this choice is interpreted as a strict preference, or different choices are made at different times and this is
taken as conclusive evidence of a change of mind and not of indifference.

8 'Values' figure in most contexts as positive, but the idea of
'disvalue' is crucial. A 'disvalue' is not simply the negation of a
positive value, but a negative value itself.

Coherence and Context

There are a number of ways in which social work values, differentiated in the above manner, could be described as forming a particular coherence. It has been assumed, for example, that coherence
and also context may be supplied by treating the values simply as the
code of practice of a particular profession. Some of the commonly
articulated values may supply the different kinds of guidance of
rules and of ideals, but a professional code provides too confined a
space for the consideration of matters of human development and
of human being. Alternatively, it may be suggested that the values
of social work should be understood as interesting variations on
themes traditional to political philosophy, namely liberty, equality
and fraternity. It is undeniable, as we have seen, that questions of
political philosophy arise in social work, but they are not simply
commensurate with the territory of social work values and they
cannot sustain the full consideration of that subject. The relationships that characterise interactions between social workers and
'clients' are not only political; the brief discussion of Lamont's view
of the comparative value judgment in Chapter 6 indicated the
difficulty of describing *the* relationship in exclusively economic or
political or juridical terms.

Another approach to the problem of discerning the form in which
the values of social work may cohere, suggests that the crucial
description is that of ideology. Frequently, it is simply assumed that
values are the equivalent of ideology or that values can only be
understood in terms of ideology. The problem with the approach is
that it repacks any distinguishable elements into 'ideology', and also
that the term 'ideology' has been used in so many different ways that
any cutting edge has long since been blunted. A recent serious
attempt to understand ideological argument as a distinctive form of

argument concluded: 'The medium of ideological communication is imagination, not analysis and proof. What the ideologically committed affirm is an aspiration of life . . . visions of human potential' (Manning (ed.), 1980, p. 130). Adopting this approach to ideology – as *visions* of human potential – would illuminate some but by no means all of the distinguishable elements to be found in 'social work values'.

The most promising approach to the problems of coherence and context which we have been considering is to consider social work in terms of a practice or grouping of practices. The notion of a practice is somewhat complex, and it differs both from 'practice' used in such conjunctions as 'the theory and practice of social work' and from more recent attempts to fuse theory and practice in the idea of praxis. I hope to develop the idea of social work as a practice in a further volume, but I want, at this stage of my argument about values, to illustrate the potential of the suggestion so that some picture may be outlined of what it means to say that the values of social work, distinguished in certain ways, form the kind of pattern associated with a practice. Fortunately, the idea of a practice has been given prominence in the recent work of Macintyre (1981) and in earlier writing by Oakeshott (1933; 1974). The connection between these two distinctive treatments has not been previously noted, as far as I know, and I will use the two approaches to outline the most important features of a practice.

Both Oakeshott and Macintyre take a wide view of a practice. For the latter neither throwing a football with skill nor bricklaying constitutes a practice, but the game of football and architecture do: 'the range of practices is wide: arts, sciences, games, politics in the Aristotelian sense, the making and sustaining of family life, all fall under the concept' (1981), p. 175). For Oakeshott practices may range from protocol to a way of life, and he lists a number of formal relationships, each of which he describes as participation in a distinguishable practice – orator and audience, the association of partners or colleagues, the relationship of husband and wife, teacher and pupil, that of speakers of a common language, of ruler and subject. These examples help to show what relationships or activities might be covered by the term 'practice', but what is it they have in common? Oakeshott believes that each of the relationships he lists

is a relationship signalled by the names of the *personae*
concerned (teacher, ruler, friend), each is capable of being

spelled out (at least in part) in terms of characteristic uses, conventions, rules, or other adverbial considerations, each is an invention of human beings, all are subject to historic vicissitudes and local variations, and none is capable of being participated in except by learning to do so. A 'neighbourly' relationship is a practice participated in, not in respect of persons living next door to one another, but in respect of their understanding themselves to be 'neighbours'. (1974, p. 57)

Macintyre attempts to define a practice through the use of a different though not unrelated group of ideas. First, he distinguishes between two kinds of good to be achieved through participation in a practice, the internal and the external: the former can only be achieved by participation in the practice, and can only be identified and recognised through the experience of participating in the practice. Second, he draws attention to the standards of excellence and obedience to rules involved in a practice: 'To enter into a practice is to accept the authority of these standards and the inadequacy of my own performance as judged by them' (1981, p. 177). Third, Macintyre argues that every practice requires a certain kind of relationship between those who participate in it, and that the types of relationship cannot be sustained without at least the virtue of truthfulness, justice and courage. The three elements in the argument are put together in a formal definition of a practice as

any coherent and complex form of socially established cooperative human activity through which goods internal to that form of activity are realised in the course of trying to achieve those standards of excellence which are appropriate to, and partially definitive of, that form of activity, with the result that human powers to achieve excellence, and human conceptions of the ends and goods involved, are systematically extended. (p. 175)

The idea of a practice is explored in this concluding chapter mainly to illustrate the possibility that social work values cohere and achieve context in the conception of a practice. Such a possibility is enhanced if we attend to some important general features of the arguments in the two writers we have been considering which can be used to illuminate the position of social work. First, the idea of a practice is far removed from any notion of practical activity as a jumble of the *ad hoc* presided over by fleeting intuition or, as Oakeshott put it in an earlier work, 'a tissue of mere conjunctions and consequently situate outside experience' (1933, p. 250). Second, the idea of a practice contradicts the view that the world of practical activity is simply raw material to be fashioned in the light of theory or theories. Macintyre stresses the idea of obedience to standards of excellence, whilst Oakeshott states, 'Practices, or the considerations they are composed of, are never "applied", they are used' (1974, p. 120). Third, a practice is not a set of detailed instructions specifying actions by some kind of routine. 'The requirements of a practice are not obeyed or disobeyed: they are subscribed to or not subscribed to. . . . A practitioner is always a performer, and this holds even in the extreme case where the practice is a ritual' (Oakeshott, 1974, pp. 58–9). Fourth, practices are procedures not processes, and procedures in which one is engaged, and both Macintyre and Oakeshott stress that to be so engaged is to participate in a tradition of practice which never exists outside the larger social traditions. This does not imply, however, any static view of the activities in question. Macintyre, for example, believes that when an institution is the bearer of a tradition of practice or practices, its common life will partly at least be constituted by continuous argument as to the nature of good practice or practices: 'Traditions, when vital, embody continuities of conflict' (1981, p. 206) Oakeshott for his part has stressed the changefulness even of activity that seeks to maintain a situation: 'To maintain is always to change. There is here, as everywhere in practical activity, an unrealised idea, an unfulfilled desire, a "to be" discrepant from "what is" ' (1933, pp. 257–8).

In this final section I have tried to illustrate from the writings of Oakeshott and Macintyre some of the central features of the description of coherent and complex human activity, or 'conduct *inter homines*' (Oakeshott, 1974, p. 57), as a practice, and also some of the interest such a description has for social workers. It is no part of these purposes to suggest in any way complete agreement between the two writers. (There is, for example, at least a tension between Oakeshott's emphasis on a tradition of practice as a collected and not a 'collective' achievement, and Macintyre's distinction between external and internal goods in terms of individual possession and the enrichment of the whole community.) Nor is it part of my intention to argue that thinking about social work as a practice provides an easy solution to the many problems involved in the description and justification of social work (It is, for example, unclear whether social work is one practice or several; nor is it obvious how the social practices that constitute modern social work might be described – as caring and tending, nurturing, saving and preserving.) What I do argue is that the potential in considering social work as a practice or grouping of practices is considerable, and that the distinguishable elements which together constitute 'social work values' are best seen and treated as elements in a practice or practices, and that the traditions of practice provide the context within which they operate.

Notes

Chapter 1: An overview

1 L.E. Elliott-Binns, *English Thought 1806-1900 — The Theological Aspect* (Longmans, 1956), points out (p. 281) 'that some of those who gave themselves up to social work did so as a way of escape from the difficulties which they felt in regard to Christianity as a doctrinal system'. C. S. Loch, some of whose ideas will be discussed in Chapter 5, advocated a 'church of charity'. Later social workers believed that to be a professional was to choose not an occupation but a distinctive way of life that would be judged 'by how we are seen to behave towards clients and towards each other' (K. McDougall, 'Obligations of a profession', *Social Work Today* 1, (1970) 20).

2 It is not easy to grasp the differences between these two approaches without falling into caricature of one or the other. Something of the difficulty of talking of results and of devotion to a process or relationship is captured in the following rather insistent excerpt of dialogue from *The Last and the First* by Ivy Compton-Burnett:

'We should be grateful for the dedication. Nothing else has the same results.'

'Results? Are we to think of them? Or to keep our minds from them as points of danger? What do you feel about it? Tell me your thoughts.'

'It is best to have good ones in anything we undertake. Or why do we undertake it?'

'And what would good ones be? What do we mean by them? What do you mean? By good ones you mean the most accepted, those that are recognised? That is what you mean?' (p. 59)

Chapter 2: The function and treatment of 'values' in social work

1 This book is devoted to an enquiry into and about social work values and into values in social work. However, it seems to me that the criticisms that can justifiably be levelled against the way in which these specific topics are treated can also be advanced in relation to social policy. Despite Hobson (quoted in Chapter 1), specific attention to 'values' in social policy is a comparatively recent development, but such attention suffers from the same limitations as are observable in social work: too much is expected of 'values' when the very idea of value and of values remains undeveloped and in a taken-for-granted state. For example, Hardy (1981) has hit on the potentially useful notion of value-contradiction, but her grasp of 'value' seems uncertain. Wilding and George (1975) believe that 'values' are important in social policy, but it is unclear from their work quite what importance they have.
2 The idea of social work or philanthropy as constituted in some form of *reconciliation* of opposites is not new. Loch, for instance, believed that 'Charity . . . represented that mood in which the opposites of thought were brought into a common view and harmonised' (C. S. Loch, 'Christian charity and political economy', *Charity Organisation Review* (N.S.) VI, (1899), 234–42). It should be noted, of course, that 'harmonisation' is different from 'balance' and tension.

Chapter 3: Conscience in social work

1 See, e.g., H. Rosenfeld, *Psychotic States*, Hogarth Press, 1965.
2 See, e.g., M. Such-Baer, 'Professional staff reaction to abortion work', *Journal of Social Casework* 55, (1974), 435–41; E. M. Smith, 'Counselling for women who seek abortion', *Social Work* (1972), 62–8.
3 Baker (1979) has recently described 'the social conscience thesis' as consisting of the following elements:

(1) Social policy manifests, through the state, the love that men have for each other. It is benevolent and is provided for the benefit of the recipients and the community as a whole.
(2) Changes in social policy result from two factors – a widening and deepening sense of social obligation, and an increase in our knowledge of need.
(3) Changes are cumulative, and policy evolves constantly though not evenly, in the direction of greater generosity and wider range.
(4) Improvements are irreversible, and contemporary services are the highest historical form.

(5) While present services are incomplete and defective, the central problems of social welfare have been solved, and society is now so constituted that we can look forward to further improvement.

4 As far as I can trace, there is no systematic treatment of conscience in the social work literature. One of the few references I can find to 'conscience' in a recent British book where it might be expected to figure concerns a brief discussion on Roman Catholics and contraception which does little more than reflect the ambiguous state of the church's mind: viz. Catholics do not agree with their church's teaching and have chosen to follow their consciences, and many of the clergy advise people to follow their own consciences as the church teaches (J. Cheetham, *Unwanted Pregnancy and Counselling*, Routledge & Kegan Paul, 1977, p. 175.) The other reference in this book, interestingly enough, is to the *doctor's* right of conscientious objection.

Chapter 4: Traditional values and neglected disvalues

1 'Coercion' is not much discussed in social work writing, and more attention should be given to the concept. Simply talking about 'coercive social workers' without attending to the complexity of the idea of coercion is insufficient. Those who would remark that they know coercion when they see it (and others) may find Nozick (1974) helpful. Nozick suggests that P coerces Q into not doing A if and only if:
   (1) P threatens to do something if Q does A, (and P knows he is making the threat).
   (2) This threat renders Q's doing A substantially less eligible as a course of conduct than not doing A.
   (3) P makes the threat in order to get Q not to do A, intending that Q realises he's been threatened by P.
   (4) Q does not do A.
   (5) P's words or deeds are part of Q's reason for not doing A.
   (6) Q knows that P has threatened to do the something mentioned in (1) if he, Q, does A.

2 See, e.g. J. Rawls, *A theory of Justice*, Harvard University Press, 1971; D. Gauthier, *Practical Reasoning*, Oxford University Press, 1963; R. Downie and E. Telfer *Respect for Persons*, Allen & Unwin, 1969; S. Darwall, 'Two kinds of respect', *Ethics* 88, (1977–8), 36-49.

Chapter 5: Three controversies

1 See C. Winnicott, *Child Care and Social Work*, Codicote Press, 1964;

N. Timms, *Social Casework: Principles and Practice* Routledge & Kegan Paul, 1964.

2 Quoted R. Gilpin, *Theory and Practice as a Single Reality*, University of North Carolina Press, 1963, p. 19.

3 What follows relies partly on the short discussion of this point in C. Kasius (ed.) (1950), p. 27

4 Some writers of the Functionalist School write more clearly than others, but even Robinson can be almost deliberately mystifying. Take, for example, the following: 'Underneath the word *control* as we examine it the word *influence* comes to mind to challenge thought as it resists understanding and definition in its usage throughout history'. These words require understanding if we are to grasp social work, but there is nothing drastically difficult in understanding 'control' and 'influence' *and* in distinguishing between them.

Chapter 6: Values, valuations and value judgments I

1 The idea of essentially contested concepts was put forward by Professor Gallie in 1956; the preference of Emmet (1979) for 'contestable' has been accepted in the present book. Emmet summarises Gallie's view of the properties of such concepts as follows: an essentially contested concept is

(1) *appraisive* in the sense that it signifies or accredits some kind of valued achievement.

(2) This achievement must be of an internally complex character, for all that worth is attributed to it as a whole.

(3) Any explanation of its worth must include reference to the respective contributions of its various parts or features, but, as these can be variously estimated, one description can set them in one order of importance and another in another.

(4) The accredited achievement admits of modification in the light of changing circumstances, and such modification cannot be prescribed in advance.

(5) When parties differ, each can recognise that his own use of the concept is contested by others, and has some appreciation of the different criteria in the light of which they are applying the concept. His own use has to be maintained against them – he uses it both aggressively and defensively. (p. 12)

References

Chapter 1: An overview

Davis, L.F. (1975), 'Touch, sexuality and power in residential settings', *British Journal of Social Work* 5, 413–22.

Fischer, J. (1976), *The Effectiveness of Social Casework*, C.C. Thomas.

Hobson, J.A. (1929), *Wealth and Life: A Study in Values*, Macmillan.

Hugman, B. (1977), *Act Natural*, Bedford Square Press.

Macintyre, A. (1981), *After Virtue: A Study in Moral Theory*, Duckworth.

Mullen, E., and Dumpson, J. (eds.) (1972), *Evaluation of Social Intervention*, Jossy Bass.

Pullan, B. (1971), *Rich and Poor in Renaissance Venice*, Blackwell.

Pumphrey, M. (1959), *The Teaching of Values and Ethics in Social Work Education*, A Project Report of the Curriculum Study, vol. XIII, Council on Social Work Education, USA.

Simpkin, M. (1979), *Trapped within Welfare*, Macmillan.

Siporin, M. (1975), *Introduction to Social Work Practice*, Collier-Macmillan.

Chapter 2: The function and treatment of 'values' in social work

Bartlett, H. (1970), *The Common Base of Social Work Practice*, National Association of Social Workers.

BASW (1977), *The Social Work Task*, Report of a BASW Working Party.

Bernstein, S. (1970), 'Values and groupwork', in *Further Explorations in Groupwork* ed. S. Bernstein, Bookstall Publications.

Bloom, M. (1975), *The Paradox of Helping*, John Wiley.

Central Council for Education and Training in Social Work (1976), *Values in Social Work*, CCETSW. Paper 13.

Channon, G. (1974), 'Values and professional social work: a field study', *Australian Social Work* 27, 5-14.

Downie, R.S., and Telfer, E. (1980), *Caring and Curing*, Methuen.

Goldstein, H. (1973), *Social Work: A Unitary Approach*, University of South Carolina Press.

Gordon, W. (1965), 'Knowledge and value: their distinction and relationship in changing social work practice', *Social Work* 10, 32-9.

Hamilton, G. (1940), *Theory and Practice of Social Casework*, Columbia University Press.

Hardy, J. (1981), *Values in Social Policy: Nine Contradictions*, Routledge & Kegan Paul.

Holme A., and Maizels, J. (1978), *Social Workers and Volunteers*, Allen & Unwin.

Kendall, K.A. (ed.) (1970), *Social Work Values in an Age of Discontent*, Council on Social Work Education, USA.

Kossal, S., and Kane, R. (1980), 'Self-determination dissected', *Clinical Social Work Journal* 8, 161–78

Latimer, E. (1978), *'The Value Components in the Everyday Life of Social Services Delivery'* Unpublished MS.

Levy, C.S. (1973), 'The value base of social work', *Journal of Education for Social Work* 9, 34–42.

Levy, C.S. (1976), *Social Work Ethics*, Human Science Press.

Lindeman, E.C. (1949), 'Science and philosophy: Sources of humanitarian faith', in *Social Work as Human Relations*, Columbia University Press.

McDermott, F. (ed.) (1975), *Self-Determination in Social Work: a collection of essays on self-determination and related concepts by philosophers and social work theorists*, Routledge & Kegan Paul.

McLeod, D. and Meyer, H. (1967), 'A study of the values of social workers', in *Behavioural Science for Social Workers*, ed. E. Thomas, Free Press.

Pearson, G. (1975), 'The politics of uncertainty: a study in the socialisation of the social worker', in *Towards a New Social Work*, ed. H. Jones, Routledge & Kegan Paul.

Pumphrey, M. (1959), *The Teaching of Values and Ethics in Social Work Education* – A Project Report of the Curriculum Study, vol. XIII, Council on Social Work Education, USA.

Rees, S. (1978), *Social Work Face to Face*, Edward Arnold.

Sainsbury, E. (1973), *Social Work with Families*, Routledge & Kegan Paul.

Siporin, M. (1975), *Introduction to Social Work Practice*, Collier-Macmillan.

Statham, D. (1978), *Radicals in Social Work*, Routledge & Kegan Paul.

Vigilante, J. (1974), 'Between values and science: education for the professional during a moral crisis or is proof truth?', *Journal of Education for Social Work* 10, 107–15.

Wilding, D. and George, V. (1975), 'Social values and social policy', *Journal of Social Policy* 4, 373–90.

Younghusband, E. (1967), *Social Work and Social Values*, Allen & Unwin.

Chapter 3: Conscience in social work

Baker, J. (1979), 'Social conscience and social policy, *Journal of Social Policy* 8, 177–206.

Broad, C. (1969), 'Conscience and conscientious action', in *Moral Concepts*, ed. J. Feinberg, Oxford University Press.

Butler's Fifteen Sermons (1970), ed. T.A. Roberts, SPCK.

Curran, C. (1975), 'Co-operation: toward a revision of the concept and its application', *Catholic Medical Quarterly*.

Dunstan, G. (ed) (1975), *Duty and Discernment*, SCM.

Dworkin, G. (1979), *Taking Rights Seriously*, Duckworth.

Emmet, D. (1958), *Function, Purpose and Power*, Macmillan.

Garnett, A. (1969), 'Conscience and conscientiousness', in *Moral Concepts*, ed. J. Feinberg, Oxford University Press.

Jones, D. (1966), 'Freud's theory of moral conscience', *Philosophy XLI*, 34–57.

Kolnai, A. (1977), *Ethics, Value and Reality*, Athlone Press.

Norman, R. (1971) *Reasons for Actions*, Blackwell.

Rieff, P. (1965), *Freud: The Mind of the Moralist*, Methuen.

Silber, J. (1969), 'Being and doing: a study of status responsibility and voluntary responsibility', in *The Anatomy of Knowledge*, ed. M. Grene, Routledge and Kegan Paul.

Towle, C. (1954), *The Learner in Education for the Professions*, University of Chicago Press.

Wand, B. (1961), 'The content and function of conscience', *Journal of Philosophy* 58, 765–72.

Wicker, B. (1976), 'Sincerity, authenticity and God', *New Blackfriars* 57, 196-203.

Chapter 4: Traditional values and neglected disvalues

Aptekar, H. (1955), *The Dynamics of Casework and Counseling*, Houghton Mifflin.

Biestek, F. (1961), *The Casework Relationship*, Allen & Unwin.

Biestek, F., and Gehrig, C. (1978), *Client Self-Determination: A Fifty Year History*, Loyola University Press.

Brager, G., and Specht, H. (1973), *Community Organising*, Columbia University Press.

Butrym, Z. (1976), *The Nature of Social Work*, Macmillan.

Central Council for Education and Training in Social Work (1976), *Values in Social Work*, CCETSW Paper 13.

Crompton, M. (1980), *Respecting Children: Social Work with Young People*, Edward Arnold.

Darwall, S. (1977/8), 'Two kinds of respect', *Ethics* 88, 36-49.

Davies, M. (1981), *The Essential Social Worker*, Heinemann.

Davison, E. (1965), *Social Casework*, Balliere, Tindall & Cox.

Downie, R.S., and Telfer, E. (1969), *Respect for Persons*, Allen & Unwin.

Downie, R.S., and Telfer, E. (1980), *Caring and Curing*, Methuen.

Dworkin, G. (1979), 'Paternalism' in *Philosophy, Politics and Society*, Fifth Series, ed. P. Laslett and J. Fishkin, Yale University Press.

Fried, C. (1970), *An Anatomy of Values: Problems of Personal and Social Choice*, Harvard University Press.

Gerard, D. (1982), *Charity and Change*, Bedford Square Press.

Gert, B. and Culver, C. (1976), 'Paternalistic behaviour', *Philosophy and Public Affairs* 6, 46-57.

Gouldner, A. (1973), *For Sociology*, Basic Books.

Husak, D. (1981), 'Paternalism and autonomy', *Philosophy and Public Affairs* 10, 27-46.

McDermott, F.E. (ed.) (1975), *Self-Determination in Social Work: A Collection of Essays on Self-determination and Related Concepts by Philosophers and Social Work Theorists*, Routledge & Kegan Paul.

National Institute for Social Work Training (1964) *Introduction to a Social Worker*, Allen & Unwin.

Nozick, R. (1974), *Anarchy, State and Utopia*, Basic Books.

Plant, R. (1970), *Social and Moral Theory in Casework*, Routledge & Kegan Paul.

Quinton, A. (1973), *The Nature of Things*, Routledge & Kegan Paul.

Rawls, J. (1972), *A Theory of Justice*, Oxford University Press.

Simpkin, M. (1979), *Trapped within Welfare*, Macmillan.

Teicher, M. (1967), 'Conclusion and summary', in *Values in Social Work: A Re-examination*, National Association of Social Workers, New York.

Towle, C. (1954), *The Learner in Education for the Professions*, University of Chicago Press.

Ware, A. (1981), 'The concept of manipulation: its relation to democracy and power', *British Journal of Political Science* 11, 163–81.

Watson, D. (1980), *Caring for Strangers*, Routledge & Kegan Paul.

Weale, A. (1978), 'Paternalism and social policy', *Journal of Social Policy* 7, 157–72.

Williams, B. (1978), 'Politics and moral character', in *Public and Private Morality*, ed. S. Hampshire, Cambridge University Press.

Chapter 5: Three controversies

Althusser, L. (1976), *For Marx*, Mospero.

Bailey, R., and Brake, M. (eds.) (1975), *Radical Social Work*, Edward Arnold.

Barnett, S. (1895), 'A Friendly Criticism of the C.O.S.', *Charity Organisation Review*, August.

Bolger, S., *et al*. (1981), *Towards Socialist Welfare Work*, Macmillan.

Bosanquet, B. (1909), 'The Report of the Poor Law Commission: The Majority Report', *Sociological Review* 11, 109–26.

Bosanquet, B. (1916), 'The Philosophy of Casework', *C.O.S. Occasional Papers* 5th Series No. 11.

Bosanquet, B. (1951), *The Philosophical Theory of the State*, Macmillan.

Brake, M., and Bailey R. (eds) (1980), *Radical Social Work and Practice*, Edward Arnold.

Brewer, C., and Lait, J. (1980), *Can Social Work Survive?*, Temple Smith.

Corrigan, P. (1975), 'Community work and political struggle', in *Sociology and Community Action*, ed. P. Leonard, *Sociological Review* Monograph No. 21.

Corrigan, P., and Leonard, P. (1978), *Social Work Practice under Capitalism*, Macmillan.

Davies, M. (1981), *The Essential Social Worker*, Heinemann.

Downie, R.S., and Telfer, E. (1980), *Caring and Curing*, Methuen.

Faatz, A. (1953), *The Nature of Choice in Casework Process*, University of North Carolina Press.

Gamble, J., (1901), 'C.O.S. Principles: The misgivings of a candid friend', *Charity Organisation Review*, March.

Galper, J. (1980), *Social Work Practice as a Single Reality*, University of North Carolina Press.

Halmos, P. (1978), *The Personal and the Political*, Hutchinson.

Hayek, F.A. (1978), *New Studies in Philosophy, Politics, Economics and the History of Ideas*, Routledge and Kegan Paul.

Hirst, P. (1975), 'Marx and Engels on law, crime and morality', in *Critical Criminology*, ed. I. Taylor *et al*., Routledge and Kegan Paul.

Hobson, J.A. (1909), *The Crisis of Liberalism*, Macmillan.

Holman, H. (1912), 'A Re-statement of First Principles of C.O.S. Work', *Charity Organisation Review*, July.

Kasius, C. (ed.) (1950), *A Comparison of Diagnostic and Functional Casework Concepts*, Family Service Association of America.

Keith-Lucas, A. (1953), 'The political theory implicit in social casework theory', *American Political Science Review* XLVII, 1076–91.

Keith-Lucas, A. (1957), *Decisions about People in Need*, University of North Carolina Press.

Loch, C.S. (1909), 'Solidarity considered as a test of social condition in England', *Charity Organisation Review*, new series XXVI, 253–67.

Maguire, J. (1978), *Marx's Theory of Politics*, Cambridge University Press.

Midgley, M. (1978), *Beast and Man: The Roots or Human Nature*, Harvester Press.

Miliband, R. (1977), *Marxism and Politics*, Oxford University Press.

Mishra, R. (1981), *Society and Social Policy: Theoretical Perspectives on Welfare*, 2nd edn. Macmillan.

Mowat, C.L. (1961), *The Charity Organisation Society, 1869-1913*, Methuen.

O'Rourke, J. (1974), *The Problem of Freedom in Marxist Thought*, Reidal Publishing Co.

Reynolds, B. (1951), *Social Work and Social Living: Explorations in Philosophy and Practice*, Citadel Press.

Richter M. (1964), *The Politics of Conscience*, Weidenfeld and Nicolson.

Robinson, V. (1930), *A Changing Psychology in Social Casework*, University of Pennsylvania Press.

Roof, M. (1972), *A Hundred Years of Family Welfare*, Michael Joseph.

Sidgwick, H. (1893), 'My Station and Its Duties', *International Journal of Ethics* 4, October.

Simpkin, M. (1979), *Trapped within Welfare*, Macmillan.

Smalley, R. (1967), *Theory for Social Work Practice*, Columbia University Press.

Statham, D. (1978), *Radicals in Social Work*, Routledge & Kegan Paul.

Stedman Jones, G. (1971), *Outcast London*, Clarendon Press.

Taft, J. (1937), 'The relation of function to process in social casework', *Journal of Social Work Process* Vol. I, no. 1.

Taft, J. (ed.) (1944), *A Functional Approach to Family Casework*, University of Pennsylvania Press.

Thompson, E.P. (1978), *The Poverty of Theory*, Merlin Press.

Townshend, Mrs (1911), *The Case against the C.O.S.*, Fabian Tract No. 158, London.

Walton, P., and Gamble A. (1972), *From Alienation to Surplus Value*, Steed & Ward.

Woodard, C. (1961), 'The Charity Organisation Society and the Rise of the Welfare State', PhD Thesis, University of Cambridge.

Woodroofe, K. (1962), *From Charity to Social Work*, Routledge & Kegan Paul.

Wootton, B. (1959), *Social Science and Social Pathology*, Allen & Unwin.

Young, A., and Ashton, E. (1956), *British Social Work in the Nineteenth Century*, Routledge & Kegan Paul.

Chapter 6: Values, valuations and value judgments I

Abercrombie, N., *et al*. (1980), *The Dominant Ideology Thesis*, Allen & Unwin.

Baier, K., and Rescher, N. (eds) (1969), *Values and The Future*, Free Press.

Barnsley, J. (1972), *The Social reality of Ethics*, Routledge & Kegan Paul.

Downie, R.S. (1980), 'The market and welfare services: remedial values', in *Social Welfare: Why and How?* ed. N. Timms, Routledge & Kegan Paul.

Downie, R.S., and Telfer, E. (1980), *Caring and Curing*, Methuen.

Emmet, D. (1979), *The Moral Prism*, Macmillan.

Frondizi, R. (1971), *What is Value?*, Open Court.

Harding, S. (1980), *On Value Systems in Europe*, Report on the preliminary Values Studies prepared for the European Values Systems Study Group, Survey Research Unit Polytechnic of North London.

Harris, C.C. (1980), *Fundamental Concepts and the Sociological Enterprise*, Croom Helm.

Hutcheon, P. (1972), 'Value theory: towards conceptual clarification', *British Journal of Sociology* 23, 172–87.

Lamont, W. (1955), *The Value Judgment*, Edinburgh University Press.

Madison, B. (1980), *The Meaning of Social Policy*, Croom Helm.

Margenau, H., and Oseanyan, F. (1970), 'A scientific approach to the theory of value', in *Human Values and Natural Science*, ed. E. Laszlo and J. Wilbur, Gordon & Breach.

Morris, C. (1956), *Varieties of Human Value*, University of Chicago Press.

Najder, Z. (1975), *Values and Evaluations*, Clarendon Press.

Oakeshott, M. (1933), *Experience and Its Modes*, Cambridge University Press, reprinted 1966.

Patterson, C. (1959), *Counselling and Psychotherapy: Theory and Practice*, Harper.

Quay, P. (1979), 'Morality by calculation of values', in *Readings in Moral Theology No.1, Moral Norms and Catholic Tradition*, ed. E. Curran and R. McCormick, Paulist Press.

Robinson, J. (1964), *Economic Philosophy*, Pelican.

Sinden, J., and Worrell, A. (1979), *Unpriced Values: Decisions without Market Prices*, John Wiley.

Smith, A. (1904), *The Wealth of Nations*, ed. E. Cannon, Methuen.

Sugden, R. (1982), *The Political Economy of Public Choice: An Introduction to Welfare Economics*, Martin Robertson.

Chapter 7: Values, valuations and value judgments II

Beehler, R. (1978), *Moral Life*, Blackwell.

Berleant, A. (1973), 'The experience and judgment of values', in *Value Theory in Philosophy and Social Science*, ed. E. Laszlo and J. Wilbur, Gordon & Breach.

Brown, J. (1976), 'The appraisal of value judgments', *Ratio XVIII*, 56–72.

Dowling, J.(n.d.), 'Conscience, love and doctrine', *Philosophical Studies* XXV, 128–47 National University of Ireland.

Downie, R.S., and Telfer, E. (1980), *Caring and Curing*, Methuen.

Emmet, D. (1958), *Facts and Obligations*, Friends of Dr William's Library, 12th Lecture, Dr Williams Trust.

Emmet, D. (1979), *The Moral Prism*, Macmillan.

Fallding, H. (1968), *The Sociological Task*, Prentice-Hall.

Findlay, J. (1970), *Axiological Ethics*, Macmillan.

Hare, R.M. (1952), *The Language of Morals*, Oxford University Press.

Hobson, J.A. (1929), *Wealth and Life: A Study in Values*, Macmillan.

Kluckhohn, C., *et al.* (1951), 'Values and value – orientations in the theory of action', in *Toward a General Theory of Action* ed. T. Parsons and E. Shils, Harvard University Press.

Margolis, J. (1971), *Values and Conduct*, Oxford University Press.

Morris, C. (1956), *Varieties of Human Value*, University of Chicago Press.

Najder, Z. (1975), *Values and Evaluations*, Clarendon Press.

Ossowska, M. (1971), *Social Determinants of Moral Ideas*, Routledge & Kegan Paul.

Phillips, D.Z., and Mounce, H.O. (1970), *Moral Practices*, Routledge & Kegan Paul.

Quinton, A. (1973), *The Nature of Things*, Routledge & Kegan Paul.

Stutchbury, O. (1973), *The Use of Principle*, Boydell Press.

Weston, M. (1975), *Morality and the Self*, Blackwell.

Williams, B. (1973), *Problems of the Self*, Cambridge University Press.

Chapter 8: Conclusions

Oakeshott, M. (1933), *Experience and Its Modes*, Cambridge University Press, reprinted 1966.

Oakeshott, M. (1974), *On Human Conduct*, Clarendon Press.

Macintyre, A. (1981), *After Virtue: A Study in Moral Theory*, Duckworth.

Manning, D. (1980), *The Form of Ideology*, Allen & Unwin.

Midgley, M. (1978), *Beast and Man: The Roots of Human Nature*, Harvester Press.

Weale, A. (1979), 'Rational choice and political principles' in *Rational Action*, ed. R. Harrison, Cambridge University Press.

Subject index

Name index

159